PRESENT AT
THE CREATION,
LEAPING IN THE
DARK, AND
GOING AGAINST
THE GRAIN

Also by Stuart Ostrow

A Producer's Broadway Journey

Thank You Very Much (The Little Guide to Auditioning for the Musical Theatre)

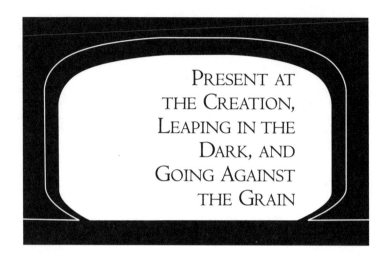

PRESENT AT
THE CREATION,
LEAPING IN THE
DARK, AND
GOING AGAINST
THE GRAIN

1776,

PIPPIN,

M. BUTTERFLY,

LA BÊTE

AND

OTHER BROADWAY

ADVENTURES

Stuart Ostrow

APPLAUSE THEATRE & CINEMA BOOKS

Present at the Creation, Leaping In the Dark, and Going Against the Grain: *1776*, *Pippin*, *M. Butterfly*, *La Bête* & Other Broadway Adventures
by Stuart Ostrow

Book cover by Mark Lerner. Book interior by Pearl Chang.

Library of Congress Cataloging-in-Publication Data:

Ostrow, Stuart 1932-
  Present at the creation, leaping in the dark, and going against the grain : 1776, Pippin, M. Butterfly, La bête, & other Broadway adventures / Stuart Ostrow.
     p.   cm.
  Includes index.
  ISBN 1-55783-646-9 (hardcover)
  1. Ostrow, Stuart, 1932-   2. Theatrical producers and directors—United States—Biography. 3. Musicals—New York (State)—New York--Production and direction.
4. Broadway (New York, N.Y.)—History. I. Title.
  ML429.O77 A3
  792.602'33'092—dc22   2005022401

Applause Theatre & Cinema Books

19 West 21st Street, Suite 201
New York, NY 10010
Phone: (212) 575-9265
Fax: (212) 575-9270
Email: info@applausepub.com
Internet: www.applausepub.com

Applause books are available through your local bookstore, or you may order at www.applausepub.com or call Music Dispatch at 800-637-2852

Sales & Distribution
North America: Europe:
  Hal Leonard Corp.   Roundhouse Publishing Ltd.
  7777 West Bluemound Road   Millstone, Limers Lane
  P. O. Box 13819   Northam, North Devon EX 39 2RG
  Milwaukee, WI 53213   Phone: (0) 1237-474-474
  Phone: (414) 774-3630   Fax: (0) 1237-474-774
  Fax: (414) 774-3259   roundhouse.group@ukgateway.net
  halinfo@halleonard.com
  Internet: www.halleonard.com

FOR ANN, FOREVER.

CONTENTS

ACKNOWLEDGMENTS

Grateful acknowledgement is made to the following newspapers and publishers, who first printed portions of the pieces specified, sometimes under different titles and in different form.

The *New York Times* Arts and Leisure Section: "Afterword."

Praeger Publishers: "Sherman Edwards and Peter Stone," "David Hirson," "Stephen Schwartz and Roger O. Hirson" "David Henry Hwang," "Frank Loesser," "Jerry Bock and Sheldon Harnick," "Meredith Willson," "Bob Dylan and Archibald MacLeish," "John Kander and Fred Ebb."

Smith & Kraus Publishers: "David Henry Hwang."

ILLUSTRATIONS AND STAGE DESIGNERS

We Take The Town, Peter Larkin, 1962,
Author's Collection.

Here's Love, William and Jean Eckart, 1963,
Author's Collection.

The Apple Tree, Tony Walton, 1966,
Author's Collection.

1776, Jo Mielziner, 1969
(from *Mielziner: Master of Modern Stage Design*
by Mary C. Henderson, Watson-Guptill Publications).

Scratch, John Conklin, 1971,
Author's Collection.

Pippin, Tony Walton, 1972,
Author's Collection.

M. Butterfly, Eiko Ishioka, 1988,
(from *Eiko on Stage*, Callaway Publishers).

La Bête, Richard Hudson, 1991,
Author's Collection.

PREFACE

I want you to know as you read me precisely who I am and what is on my mind. I want you to understand exactly who you are getting: you are getting a man who for some time now has felt radically separated from most of the ideas that seem to interest the Mafiosi of success and failure of the Great White Way. The forces suppressing quality musical theatre today are: the Broadway establishment, preferring to buy the future rather than undertake the labor of making it, and the conservative constituency in the National Endowment for the Arts (NEA) who insist musical theatre is not high culture and therefore should be relegated to a lower level of federal recognition and financial support. It is vital to do battle against both, for they are grievously in error.

Let's start with the Feds. The dangerous proposition in the air, originated by the arts-conservatives, is to the effect that the NEA should divorce the shotgun administration of opera and musical theatre and return opera to the Music Program whence it came and where it belongs. These appointees to The National Council on the Arts, who review and make recommendations to the Chairman on applications for grants, funding guidelines, and leadership initiatives, consider themselves the guardians of opera's treasury and imply its coupling with musical theatre is akin to a mixed marriage, where the chances of a lasting union are doomed and its progeny is to be cursed. Because I am a musician, have produced and directed new Broadway musicals, am a founding panel member of the NEA's

opera-musical program and have been happily mixed-married to the same woman for forty-eight years, I feel qualified to attempt to neutralize their intellectual prejudice.

Why can't we live together? Will *Porgy and Bess, Candide, Sweeney Todd,* or *Einstein on the Beach,* diminish an opera audience's passion for *Fidelio* or *Montezuma?* Hardly. What upsets the preservers of the past most about our consanguinity is the fear we will produce hybrid, inferior musical works instead of the "treasures of civilization," past operatic masterpieces, and will continue to neglect the genius of our own twentieth-century composers: Douglas Moore, Virgil Thomson, Samuel Barber, Howard Hanson, Roger Sessions, Carlisle Floyd and Aaron Copland. They speak clearly about the lack of lasting American art since the end of World War II, but are disingenuous when suggesting it has something to do with breeding; they ridicule the possibility that opera and musical theatre artists could discover creative common ground. The truth is their interest in the musical is limited, and their opinion of Broadway is that it represents at best an uneasy marriage between musicians of generally serious background and the lure of show-business fame. Opera remains an elite form, European and in some sense romantic in origin, belonging in large measure to the domain of high culture and recalling the past rather than mirroring contemporary daily life. No room in their opinion for Gershwin, Rodgers, Sondheim, Porter, Bernstein, Kern, Berlin, Loesser, or Weill. No room for the indigenous American art form, yesterday or today.

There's much that's quixotic about Federal funding for the arts; I agree with John Updike when he stated in the *New York Times*: "I would rather have as my patron a host of anonymous citizens digging into their own pockets for the price of a book or a maga-

zine than a small body of enlightened and responsible men and women administering public funds."

Which brings me to the Broadway bureaucracy. Landlords and corporate interests that dominate Broadway are concerned with money to get power and power to protect the money, a creed epitomized by the Medici. However unlike the family that boosted Florence to years of calm in which the Renaissance could flower, today's faux scions tithe musical cartoons, puppet shows, and live motion pictures as an alternative to commissioning creative monuments to the human spirit. Once upon a time America was creating things, not only the stuff for everyday life, but also fantasy, myths, ritual, and catharsis for the soul, albeit in a dark theatre. Sure the business of America was business but sometimes a Broadway drama or musical would transform you. The world was full of meaning. Exactly when was the world emptied of substance? Exactly when did the images lose their color? I have mixed emotions about having created the *Pippin* commercial I put on television in 1973. The commercial was the first of its kind, and a minute of lightning in a bottle, but it never occurred to me it would change the way theatre was to be produced. From that moment on hucksters could sell musicals as soap, so long as their spot had glitter and hype. Never mind producing a great show, produce a great commercial! Everyone became a theatre impresario overnight: lawyers, landlords, investment bankers, motion picture moguls, dilettantes, and a precious few genuinely talented young producers. Oscar Hammerstein II, remembering Theresa Helburn of the Theatre Guild put it this way at her eulogy: "I think only people in the theatre know what a producer is. The public does not know. It knows a writer writes, and an actor acts, and a director tells them what to do. A producer raises money. Well, he does, and in some cases that's all he does. But the workers in the the-

atre know that this is not the real thing. A producer is a rare, para-doxical genius—hard-headed, soft-hearted, cautious, reckless, a hopeful innocent in fair weather, a stern pilot in stormy weather, a mathematician who prefers to ignore the laws of mathematics and trust intuition, an idealist, a realist, a practical dreamer, a sophisticat-ed gambler, a stagestruck child. That's a producer."

Forty-four years ago promising oneself not to keep his dreams within reason was a reasonable credo for an aspiring young man. Today it is the exception. Today the theatre is ruled by bottom-line thinking. Who's the star? What does it cost? When will it recoup? Where is the profit-earnings ratio? How will it play in Nutley and Nagasaki? In these meretricious times when many incip-ient theatrical talents seek refuge in Comedy Central, MTV, Las Vegas, Hollywood, or quit altogether, looking for new writers, plays and musicals and producing them is the best solution for keeping the fabulous invalid alive. The nonprofit theatre is not the answer. Their struggle for subsidies and grants limit the gamble they will take on new works, especially musicals and expensive plays, and there are warning signs the conservatives in Government will require the right of censorship before administering any funds.

The individual entrepreneur, the lone gun, the stubborn independent, has always been our best hope. Feuer and Martin, Leland Hayward, Mike Todd, Robert Fryer, Cheryl Crawford, Hal Prince, David Merrick, Richard Barr, Robert Stigwood, Joe Papp, Binkie Beaumont, Michael Codron, and Cameron Mackintosh, are the remarkable and woefully few that span the decades. Successful new producers will attract unconventional capital investment, there-by reducing the landlord's influence in the theatre, and will possibly stem the cultural malaise that began with their reign thirty-three years ago. Sensing the lack of producers in the 1970s, directors,

authors, and actors produced their own work and with too few exceptions failed. Not until the balance between theatre owners and producers is restored (the so-called League of American Theatres and Producers is a front for theatre owners) and the thrust of production is to create new works will we have a vibrant, healthy commercial theatre.

Finally, what can be said about the place we need to be? We need a new salon where unique works are produced, where writers can compare, debate, and challenge the pain and passion of creating original musicals, operas, and perhaps yet undiscovered theatrical forms. Why not create a Cradle, a place of origin and continuity where first-time dramatists and songwriters are nurtured, and whose original works are ultimately produced on, and beyond Broadway? We need to teach the student writer to dramatize action, inspire the incipient novelist, poet, and journalist to create insight and humor through lyrics and librettos, and encourage the new composer of MTV, opera, and minimalist music to fuse with the art of telling stories. If enough marriages can be nurtured between these crossover worlds, we will begin to illuminate the human condition for a vast audience. It might even produce some stagestruck children who will grow up ignoring the bottom line, and risk everything. There was a time on Broadway when theatre was a shot fired around the world, and it would change your life, and it happened at least once every season, and once was enough.

INTRODUCTION

Creativity always came as a surprise to me; therefore I could never count on it and dared not believe in it until it had happened. To deal with uncertainty I had enough faith in the future to take risks—a musical about the signing of the Declaration of Independence, a drama concerning a Chinese transvestite communist spy and a French diplomat, a comedy of manners in rhymed couplets, and an unlikely musical set in Charlemagne's Holy Roman Empire. Faith makes the earth move, evokes commitments; risk propels adventure and innovation. A theatre ruled by faith and risk rather than rational calculus, will call forth an endless stream of invention and art. Agnes De Mille insisted, "Living is a form of not being sure, not knowing what next or how. The moment you know you begin to die a little. The artist never entirely knows. We guess. We may be wrong but we take leap after leap in the dark." Similarly, going against the grain is life giving but it doesn't endear me to the establishment. Being an independent producer makes the journey lonelier and tougher, but not tipping my soul to the system allows me to arrive at the end of the road with my integrity on.

It sounded like a wisecrack when Frank Loesser told me: "A producer is someone who knows a writer." Little did I realize it would remain the constant instruction I would abide by for all my Broadway productions. To understand the relationship between the producer and the creators of a musical one must plumb the mystery of *collaboration*. Marriage is easy. Collaboration is hard. Theatre

demands it. Egos must be bridled to allow the director, choreographer, composer, lyricist, book writer, designer, or producer—whoever has the best idea at the time—to lead the pursuit for artistic truth. Ultimately it is the writer who must decide if and how his work is altered. For a writer, success is always temporary, only a delayed failure. And it is incomplete. There are faults in the work, which only the writer detects; even his or her unfavorable critics miss them, dwelling on obvious points, which can be repaired, but like a skilled intuitive builder he or she can sniff out the dry rot in the beams, but seldom has the courage to dismantle the whole house and start again. That's when the producer arrives to gull, cull, and diddle them into rewriting. The Irish playwright Sean O'Casey said this about writing plays: "They're a heart-scald when you're writing them and they become a terror during rehearsals." Here then are the untold (some twice-told but in greater detail) present at the creation stories about *Pippin*, by Stephen Schwartz and Roger O. Hirson, *1776*, by Sherman Edwards and Peter Stone, *La Béte*, by David Hirson, and *M. Butterfly*, by David Henry Hwang, along with personal reflections of my adventures with other playwrights and songwriters from mid-century to the millennium; evidence regarding the unique theatre process of the passing of clay between the originators in order to form a more perfect creation.

1

FRANK LOESSER

GUYS AND DOLLS
THE MOST HAPPY FELLA
HOW TO SUCCEED IN BUSINESS
WITHOUT REALLY TRYING

When I started out as Frank Loesser's apprentice in addition to his defining what a producer was ("someone who knows a writer"), he also decreed that "loud is good" and "work in the theatre because you'll always have someplace to go after dinner." Armed with these commandments I began my Broadway journey. There were dozens of young producers trying their wings in the fifties, which is one reason why the theatre soared. I made my way into the legitimate theatre at twenty-two working for Frank and being a trained musician (clarinetist) in search of a career. My music education brought me closer to understanding the composer's goals. Writers trusted my instincts and editing their songs was not only fun, it was creative. That's when I decided, if you can't write, produce. For the moment, however, I had to be content helping to find, publish, and plug hit songs for the Frank Music Corp.: "Unchained Melody," "Cry Me a River," "The Twelfth of Never," and "Yellowbird," made me a contender.

Yip Harburg said, "Music makes you feel a feeling, words make you think a thought. A song makes you feel a thought." And, I said to myself, it takes a creative producer to nurture a good one and present it to the public. So obeying Loesser's first commandment, I began cultivating both fledging and veteran theatre writers: Norman Gimbel, Hugh Martin and Ralph Blaine, Ogden Nash and Vernon Duke, Oscar Brown, Jr., Lew Spence, Marilyn and Alan Bergman, Arthur Hamilton, Jerry Livingston and Paul Francis Webster, Alex North, Rod McKuen, Jay Livingston and Ray Evans, Hoagy Carmichael, Sammy Cahn and James Van Heusen, Mark McIntyre, Bob Wells, Sammy Fain, David Amram, Milton Schafer, Lee Pockriss and Hal David, Peter Udell, Robert Waldman and Alfred Uhry, Hy Zaret and Lou Singer, Charles Gaynor, Phil Springer, Ervin Drake, Julie Mandel, Fran Landesman and Tommy Wolf, Richard Lewine and Arnold Horwitt, Richard Maltby and David Shire, Billy Goldenberg,

Bob James and Jack O'Brien, and Helen Deutsch. What an apprenticeship!

Frank never trusted producers, which was the reason he established Frank Productions Inc., the Broadway co-producers of *The Most Happy Fella*, *The Music Man*, *Greenwillow*, and *How to Succeed in Business Without Really Trying*. Also as the music publisher of *The Pajama Game* and *Kismet*, Frank tortured *Pajama Game* producer Freddie Brisson, Rosalind Russell's husband, nicknaming him, "The lizard of Roz," and then he set his sights on Ed Lester. Edwin Lester, the producer of *Kismet*, originated the Los Angeles Civic Light Opera Association in the 1940s as a booking house for touring Broadway musicals. Ed Lester and Frank Loesser lived in the same New York hotel penthouse floor during the run of *Kismet*, much to Loesser's displeasure. Lester's archconservative audience had compelled him to censor some of Loesser's *Guys and Dolls* lyrics for the road company's tour in Los Angeles, and Frank wanted revenge. As a result, guests who visited Loesser were told to first ring Lester's adjacent suite doorbell and ask if it was Frank Loesser's apartment. Edwin Lester was furious and decided to ask Loesser to stop the harassment. One day, sharing a jam-packed elevator, Lester sidled close to Loesser and whispered: "You're a great songwriter, Frank, and I'm a respected producer; why can't we act like colleagues?" Without missing a beat Loesser shouted: "If you touch me again I'll call a cop! And where is my laundry?" Everyone except Frank and I got off at the next floor. When I left Frank in 1961, he admonished me that producers come and go but copyrights were forever. He was right of course and when in 1994 the late William Henry III, *Time* magazine drama critic described me as an endangered species, I thought it was a cheerless tribute and remembered that Frank Music Corp. was sold to CBS for millions.

My Broadway journey began when I was a student in Manhattan's High School of Music & Art and my first big date was with a knockout cello player who was also a devotee of Broadway musicals. She bought two balcony seats to *Guys and Dolls* for my birthday and we sat mesmerized watching and listening to a trio of horseplayers sing, "Fugue for Tinhorns," then a Salvation Army chorale imploring gamblers to "Follow the Fold." The show was a flood of surprising, funny songs—canons and gospels, sexy, gymnastic dances, thrilling orchestration and vocal arrangements—and a new language, where Hotbox strippers tell their boyfriends to take back their "poils," because they're not one of those "goils." At the final curtain I was hopelessly in love. Not so much with the knockout cello player as with the Broadway musical. And when as a twenty-one year old buck sergeant in the United States Air Force in 1953, producer/director of various camp Shows, and weekly network radio broadcasts during our "Korean Police Action," my love affair with *Guys and Dolls* paid off.

The Air Force wanted a morale building National Stage Show along the lines of Irving Berlin's *This Is the Army* and Moss Hart's *Winged Victory* to commemorate the fiftieth anniversary of powered flight, and they asked me to produce it. I convinced the Colonel in charge that professional writers were needed (Frank Loesser of course) and hitched a C-54 ride to Mitchell AFB in Long Island. I gave the elevator man at Manhattan's Warwick Hotel twenty bucks to tell me what floor Mr. Loesser was on, and rang the doorbell in the tower suite. It was a payoff that changed my life. Looking like a small dapper Anthony Quinn, and as warm and funny and smart as anyone I have ever known, Frank Loesser invited me in and we drank up the night. We exchanged loop-to-loop concepts for the Air Force musical and I swear he even wrote a lyric

for a General who gambled: "Old crap-shooters never die, they just stay faded," he ad-libbed at the piano. After a couple of deals before dawn, Frank announced he would write the score, only if I hired Abe Burrows to write the book. Was I dreaming? I had lunch the next day with Burrows at the 21 Club, and was back in Washington, D.C. that afternoon with an agreement from two Broadway giants—the creators of *my* Guys and Dolls, to write the USAF *Conquest of the Air*. The colonel thought I was a genius and gave me a three-day pass.

The following week I was told to appear before the Senate Government Operations Committee's Permanent Subcommittee on Investigations. I was asked what my political affiliations were, was I ever a member of the Labor Party, wasn't my father born in Kiev, Russia? It was frightening. What did this have to do with putting on a show for the Air Force? It wasn't until my Colonel vouched for me and explained that McCarthyism was in the air—synonymous with political opportunism and public character assassination—and that Abe Burrows was under investigation for alleged Communist sympathy, that I realized what Loesser's intention was. If the United States Air Force would hire Burrows, the witch hunt would stop. It was why Frank agreed to write the musical, giving up a year of his life and putting his reputation on the line. It was called friendship. In the end my chicken Colonel wouldn't fight the barnyard cocks and I had to tell Frank Loesser and Abe Burrows the Air Force couldn't use them. "You're a born producer, kid," Frank said. "And when you get out of the service, you've got a job." Sure enough after my release from the service, Loesser's Frank Music Corp. hired me and I worked my way up the ladder from song-plugger to press agent to governor general of the Hollywood office to vice-president and General Professional Manager of the New York headquarters at twenty-eight.

After seven shaping years with Frank Music Corp., culminating with *How to Succeed in Business Without Really Trying*, I flew to London to tell Loesser I was going to leave as Vice-President and General Manager of FMC and produce my first solo musical, *We Take the Town*. He was annoyed but smiled and said: "What the hell, I've had the best years of your life, and remember…" "I know Frank," I recited, "a producer is someone who knows a writer." PS: The next day a new Mason & Hamlin grand piano was delivered to our East End apartment along with a check for $10,000.00 (a lot of money in 1961) with a handwritten note that simply, yet grandiloquently, said: "Dear Stu: I believe in you, Love Frank." I like to think there was enough of J. Pierrepoint Finch in me to have earned Frank's farewell.

Frank Loesser was all about taking chances, never allowing himself to become too comfortable with subject, tone, rhythm, or syntax, unlike Alan Jay Lerner, who after *My Fair Lady* and *Gigi* said he had "found his sound." Loesser leaped from the English farce of *Where's Charley?*, to the Manhattan mugs of *Guys and Dolls*, and to the Napa Valley sweethearts of *The Most Happy Fella*. His genius for writing authentic lyrics and muscular music set the tone of *Guys and Dolls* by having its Broadway denizens sing in Runyonesque patois. In the first four bars of "Fugue for Tinhorns," Loesser has Nicely Nicely Johnson reading and singing from a racing form establishing the character's métier. Bennie Southstreet adds more bookie lingo and Rusty Charlie verifies the show's New York City locale by citing one of its 1950 daily newspapers. For this fugue Loesser composed a more complicated canon than "Frere Jaques," but the musical satisfaction of listening to three separate stories with the same overlapping melody was just as enjoyable. Phrases such as "feed box noise," "no bum steer," and, "a handicapper that's real sincere," came straight from the horse's mouth and transported us into fable.

Guys and Dolls director George S. Kaufman was the celebrated author of *Once in a Lifetime*, *You Can't Take it With You*, and *The Man Who Came to Dinner*. A member of the legendary Algonquin Round Table, Kaufman was known for the destructive wisecrack, the verbal ricochet, and it was never more resonant than when fledgling book writer Abe Burrows proudly boasted "Fugue for Tinhorns" would take place on a treadmill. "Isn't that great, George?" asked Abe, breathlessly. Deadpan, Kaufman replied: "That depends upon what they are saying on the treadmill, Mr. Burrows." Burrows never asked Kaufman another question. Another tense moment was addressed when Kaufman, Loesser, and producer Cy Feuer took a taxicab ride to New Jersey in order to see Jo Mielziner's set being built. The cabby zoomed through downtown onto the West Side Highway, running three red lights and nearly mowing down an old lady. The passengers were silent with fear and not a word had been spoken until the George Washington Bridge came into sight. At that moment, taciturn Kaufman gently tapped the crazed driver on the shoulder: "See that bridge, driver?" asked Kaufman; "Yeah, so what?" the driver sneered. Kaufman leaned over and whispered into his ear: "Don't cross it until you to come to it."

"Follow the Fold" starts off as a typical Salvation Army hymn when Sister Sarah and her group pray. Then an unexpected afterthought—an extra pick-up bar leading back to the chorus makes us laugh. In another parody, "The Oldest Established," guys sing of the Biltmore garage wanting a grand and not having a grand on hand, being a good scout, looking for action even when the heat is on; then joining in pious harmony to sing an oxymoron in tribute to the oldest established permanent floating crap game in New York. In "Adelaide's Lament," the character gets her tips from a medical journal rather than a racing form, and diagnoses her cold symptoms are

being caused by too many postponed wedding dates. It remains a classic comic turn for broads with a Bronx accent.

"My Time of Day" is a soliloquy wherein we're given a glimpse into the character's soul; in this case a surprisingly poetic one hidden within a mug's demeanor. Sky Masterson is the most adventurous gambler on the street; he has won his bet he could get prim and proper Salvation Army Sarah to Havana to spend the night with him. Now that she's had too much to drink, he sings to her about the rain washed pavement and street lamps filling the gutter with gold. Then for the clincher he tells her she's the only doll he's ever wanted to share with him... and wins the doll and the bet. It also gave Loesser another chance to compose a beautiful melody with difficult intervals, ninths, as he did before with the popular standard, "Spring Will Be a Little Late this Year." "More I Cannot Wish You," the show's charm song, was given to beloved vaudevillian, Pat Rooney Sr., who plays fairy Godfather to Sarah, and wishes her a lover.

One final untold story regarding *Guys and Dolls*, this one about the movie version. Hollywood adaptations of hit Broadway musicals, with too few exceptions, fail. Why? For openers, you don't photograph sweat, the crucial result of energy on stage. Whereas it is the theatre's aim to transform commentary into dramatic action, films indulge in reaction shots and romantic close-ups. Stage scenery is an abstraction, movies love panoramic reality. The most difficult transition to overcome, however, is the movie star. Samuel Goldwyn's movie of *Guys and Dolls* was no exception and brought Frank head to head with another Frank—Sinatra—who insisted on crooning "Sue Me," Nathan Detroit's half-spoken begrudging apology to Adelaide for postponing yet another wedding date. At the prerecording session when Loesser heard Sinatra's romantic gliding and sliding from one pitch to another along with the throbbing string section accompani-

ment, he stopped the session and belted him, right in front of Goldwyn and director Joe Mankiewicz. Loesser was banned from the set, which is why Marlon Brando, who was playing Sky Masterson, wound up with Loesser's new hit song, "A Woman In Love," originally intended for Sinatra.

In April 1956, both *My Fair Lady* and *The Most Happy Fella* were trying out in Philadelphia, on route to Broadway. Frank Loesser and I went to the Erlanger Theatre to see the Lerner and Loewe musical and check out the competition. It was clearly a box office bonanza and one of the best musicals ever produced. Frank turned to me after the final curtain and said: "The pain is plain and mainly in my brain; I think they've got it."

When we opened out of town and the critics hailed *The Most Happy Fella*, as a "brilliant new American opera," Loesser was horrified that the highbrow tone of the notices would scare away traditional Broadway audiences. "Call the press, Ostrow, and tell 'em we're not an opera for God's sake; we're a ...Loessercal!" Ironically, Frank was insecure about his lack of music education notwithstanding his great Broadway successes; brought about, in part, by his perceived position in the Loesser family. His older brother, Arthur, was a celebrated pianist and an academician, and his mother, a cultured matriarch who thought being a Tin Pan Alley songwriter was meretricious. All the more astonishing this self-taught composer was able to create a seminal opera/musical comedy/dramatico-musical work, which has endured and promises to be around now and forever.

The truth is, the score for *The Most Happy Fella* is a cornucopia of operatic arias ("My Heart Is so Full of You"), Hit Parade songs ("Standing on the Corner") and other musical expressions that cannot be defined. "Ooh! My Feet!" is just such a phenomenon. Rather than a flashy-happy opening number danced and sung by a

chorus of Broadway gypsies, Loesser begins the musical with a solitary barefoot waitress massaging her sore foot. Possibly because Susan Johnson had a voice like a room full of cellos, or due to the sheer impertinence of the song, audiences stopped the show each performance when she finished counting her toes. I first met my wife-to be, Ann Gilbert, on the opening night of *The Most Happy Fella*, in the Imperial Theatre lobby and was in love with her by the second act. Which may explain why I well up each time I hear "Somebody, Somewhere," a beautiful soprano lament setting the musical's operatic tone, then "Big D," and "I Like Everybody," which had little to do with the plot but were vastly entertaining and written as contrast to the seriousness of the entire work.

It is testimony to Frank Loesser's immense talent that *The Most Happy Fella*, never broke down with schizophrenia. In a sense Loesser wrote enough music for two shows—ballads: "Joey, Joey, Joey," "Don't Cry," "Warm All Over; choral numbers: "The Most Happy Fella," "Sposalizio," " Fresno Beauties," "How Beautiful the Days," "Song of a Summer Night,"; arias: "A Long Time Ago," "Plenty Bambini," "Young People," "I Know How It Is," "Aren't You Glad?" "I Don't Like this Dame," "Like a Woman Loves a Man," "Please Let Me Tell You"; duets: "Happy to Make Your Acquaintance," "Cold and Dead"; trios: "Abbondanza," "Benvenuta," and "Nobody's Ever Gonna Love You"—prompting Columbia Records to record its first three-set original cast album, at a running time of 134:12.

The anecdote: Morley Meredith was originally cast as Joe, but after the Boston opening Loesser wanting a pop voice to croon "Don't Cry" and "Joey, Joey, Joey," sent for Art Lund, a former Benny Goodman band singer to replace him for the Philadelphia opening. Meredith didn't have an adequate understudy and the

producers fearing he would find out he was being replaced and quit before Lund was ready to go on, rehearsed Lund in the Warwick Hotel ballroom far away from the Shubert Theatre. It was a mad rush to get him in the part, so on opening night when Lund was supposed to sing about the wind *smelling of Oregon cherries*, Art sang *smelling of ordinary women*. The next day the *Philadelphia Inquirer* wrote: "Art Lund's delivery of, 'Joey, Joey, Joey,'" was thrilling, with the exception of one lapse of taste which should have been banned in Boston."

Frank was an intensely private person and he hated publicity. "Lettuce and the press are the enemy," he maintained and seldom gave any interviews or appeared in public. That private life included a troubled marriage with Lynn Loesser, a devoted father relationship with his children, Susan and John, and making furniture in the woodshed in back of his North Arden Beverly Hills home. I remember one night in Las Vegas, Loesser and I going to the Sands Hotel to pay our dues to The Four Lads (they had made a hit recording of "Standing On The Corner") and the moment when they appeared singing: *Frank Loesser!/Frank Loesser!/Frank Loesser!/*—the introduction to a song tribute of all of his hits, coincidental with a spotlight focused in our ringside table—Frank pulled me by the sleeve and bolted into the lobby. "Did you know about this?," he bellowed in earshot of the performance inside. When I tried to shush him he opened both doors leading into the theatre shouting : **And tell The Four Gonads I have a private life!"**

Greenwillow was Loesser's flop; a kinder gentler, bucolic musical, which he lavished with a haunting score. It sang of teakettles, Clegg's old cow, and summertime love. The book didn't work and Frank said: "It's the last time I put a pink sequined gown on a girl who hasn't bathed."

At first, Frank Loesser didn't want to write the score to *How to Succeed in Business Without Really Trying*. "I've done my wiseguy show," he told *Guys and Dolls* producers Cy Feuer and Ernie Martin. Frank was wary of "Cy and Ernie," (he said their names sounded like a Japanese goodbye) and now they were nipping at his heels to repeat his successful collaboration with Abe Burrows. who was set to write and direct *How to Succeed*. Loesser thought his next project should be more challenging. "I've never rhymed in Russian; how about a musical *Potemkin*, and *Catherine The Great?*" *Pleasures and Palaces* (directed by Bob Fosse and closed out of town before reaching Broadway) would be written years later. I believe the only reason he ultimately decided to write *Succeed* was in order to help Burrows have a much-needed hit. It wasn't the first time he put his career on the line for his friend, Abe.

Robert Morse was a sensation as Finch, and the production's cartoon-styled satire of the corporate world produced Bob Fosse's comical take on how desperate employees can get for their "Coffee Break." Loesser's shrewd perception of the executive mentality was humorously on target in "The Company Way," an employee's hymn dedicated to playing it safe. In a breezy, conversational, uniquely Loesser duet, Twimble instructs Finch how to survive. It can be said, Twimble was the first employee to anticipate the management downsizing of corporate America.

"*A Secretary is Not a Toy*" will remain frozen in politically correct amber, as a reminder of those quaint days when harassment law suits came only from the Internal Revenue Service, not the girls at the office. God, did Loesser have fun with pointing out she was not a toy, and definitely not employed to do a gavotte with the boss. Despite Bob Fosse's 12/8 dance break, it was written as a waltz dedicated to all of Frank's secretaries whom he adored; from Betty Good to

Margie Gans and beyond. Irving Berlin's secretary was Mynna Dryer, and music publisher Buddy Norris was lucky to have Silvia Herscher to look after Jerry Herman, Adams and Strouse, and Cy Coleman. A legion of these dedicated women ran the business with little thought of breaking through the glass ceiling. Although today's women have joined the CEO ranks, what hasn't changed is the ego of the self-absorbed executive. Male or female, looking into a mirror and singing "I Believe in You," they still imagine themselves as invincible. (Think Patricia Russo or Carly Fiorina.) It was a self-love song, releasing pent-up chutzpa with religious fervor and was to become the theme song for the likes of Bill Gates and Steve Jobs waiting in the wings.

Note: *How to Succeed* won the Tony Award as best musical and established a malignant precedent by splitting the award in to two parts, best book and best score. For too many years the establishment has asked voters to dismember musicals. Surely the purpose of collaboration is to create a seamless artistic work and to separate the results is akin to birthing a baby and awarding prizes for best mother and best father. It profits a man nothing to give his soul for the whole world...but for a Tony?

Frank had a terrible temper and a wicked tongue, which he tried to keep in check, not always with success. He called Sam and Bella Spewack a new fish dish and when lawyers Arnold Weissberger and Howard Reinheimer asked Frank whose name should come first, now that they were establishing a new law firm, Frank replied: "Call yourselves 'The Wisenheimers.'" Then there was the time, leaving his Park Avenue apartment house during a sirocco rain, when a taxi appeared on the downtown side of Park. We ran across the island to the opposite street (getting soaked to the skin) and when Frank finally reached the taxi and pulled the door open, we saw a wizened

old lady bent over in the back seat. "Sit up you cocksucker!" Frank roared, slamming the door on a shaken octogenarian.

The last time I saw Frank was at Jo Loesser's invitation. He was dying of lung cancer and she was thoughtful enough to ask if I wanted to say goodbye. *Of course I didn't want to say goodbye*, but I went to his hospital chamber of horrors anyway and found Frank with tubes in his nose, transfusions in his arms, and terror in his eyes. He was only fifty-nine. Seated at the edge of his bed I tried some small talk, about my new hit musical *1776*, our new Pound Ridge home, second daughter Kate and expectant son, John, but Frank would have none of it. Silence. Having not said a single word he turned away from me. Not out of incivility, I think, but perhaps because in the past when we spoke he could make me laugh, cause me to feel smarter than I was, and serve as my role model. He was the father I never had, and I was the son he never had and it was over.

2

MATT DUBEY AND HAROLD KARR

WE TAKE THE TOWN

MEL BROOKS

ALL AMERICAN
THE PRODUCERS

After *How to Succeed*, I left Frank Loesser to produce my first solo musical, *We Take the Town*, starring Robert Preston as the legendary Pancho Villa. His critics assassinated Villa in Mexico City in 1923 while we were merely slaughtered in 1962 when we opened in Philadelphia. Nevertheless I loved the character, as he was a youthful, romantic idealist who achieved power then disintegrated into incompetence. It wasn't Dubey and Karr's fault, they had written a brilliant Mexican mariachi score—vindication after an unpromising debut with Ethel Merman and *Happy Hunting*—and because of their intimidating experience with the star, made me promise to cast an unknown as the female lead. Barbra Streisand knocked me out in 1961 when she was performing at The Blue Angel and asked to audition for *We Take the Town*, opposite Preston. "The part calls for an aristocratic Mexican lady, " I said, somewhat apprehensively. "So what," she replied; "When I sing, there is no nationality." I was sold, but Preston wanted a straight actress and turned me down. (Ironically, Barbra recorded "How Does The Wine Taste," from our score, and of course, she was right.)

A more experienced producer would not have chosen Alex Segal to direct but Preston insisted on rehearsals beginning in a month's time and I was panic stricken. (Bob had a movie offer for *How the West Was Won*, so if we were a flop he would be available.) *We Take the Town* was a musical about the Mexican revolution, designed by Peter Larkin in earth colors—mostly orange—and I knew I was in trouble when Segal, upon seeing the completed set, screamed, "I told Larkin, I hate orange!" Kermit Bloomgarden, co-producer of *The Music Man*, attended our out of town opening and urged Preston to bolt the show (not his most collegial moment) but Jerry Robbins came to my rescue the day after premiering *Oh Dad, Poor Dad;* he loved the show and agreed to replace Segal. Furthermore, my benefactor,

Goddard Lieberson, the head of Columbia Records, had invested $350,000 (the entire capitalization) and offered to put up whatever more it cost to get the show to Broadway. As it turned out, Robbins collapsed during rehearsals and I had an ambulance take him back to East 81st Street in Manhattan. (Five years later Jerry Robbins became my theatre conscience, asking me to run his American Theatre Lab and negotiate an agreement with all the theatrical unions for the creation of The New York Public Library for the Performing Arts on Film and Tape archives.) Robbins urged me to take over the direction but Preston would not agree, so that night, I closed the musical and threw a farewell party for the company. The generosity of my colleagues, however, turned what should have been despair into hope. Meredith Willson flew from Los Angeles to Philadelphia and played the score to *Here's Love.* "Your next musical, Stu," he announced in our crowded, flop hotel room.

When I returned to New York the first phone call was from Stephen Sondheim, who asked if I would send him the music to "Silverware," the song he admired from the aborted production. It gave me another reason not to give up. The best moment came when John Shubert, the remaining scion of the family theatre empire, returned my $20,000 deposit for the Broadway Theatre, with this note: "Try again, kid, we need new producers." *We Take the Town* was a musical adapted from the MGM film *Viva Villa!* Starring Wallace Beery and a lot of horses. It was the precursor to the Kazan/Brando *Viva Zapata*, and was filmed in Mexico with a hundred bandit-extras shooting up every Federale in sight. Our musical could never replicate the cinematic realism of the Mexican Revolution.

When we were trying out at the Shubert Theatre in Philadelphia, Mel Brooks was the book writer for another new musical, *All American*, starring Ray Bolger and directed by Joshua Logan at

the Erlanger Theatre down the block. Both shows were in deep trouble and Mel and I commiserated. "Logan is a crazy lady," Brooks would scream, "Every time we try to fix a number, instead of rehearsing, he has those idiot producers bring a five-course meal from Bookbinders restaurant to the theatre and we all have to watch him eat! I'm not a writer, I'm a *waiter.*" Perhaps you can understand why seven years later Mel wrote and directed his classic film-spoof *The Producers* and didn't write anything for the stage until thirty-five years later, when he cashed in his movie and gave us a new Shylock and Fagin for the millennium. Having spent the past forty-two years producing on Broadway, proud of my Jewish heritage, and more often than not having enriched my loyal investors, I am here today not to praise Brooks but to bury him.

"We don't talk about Joe," my Aunt Florence said, "He's meshugganah." When I was twelve, my cousin, Joe Plotz, serving with the 505th Parachute Infantry Regiment, 82nd Airborne Division, was captured during the Battle of the Bulge in 1944. He suffered a nervous breakdown and after V. E. Day was sent back to the States, where he was placed in a military hospital for the insane. I was angry we weren't allowed to see him, and asked sarcastically: "In other words, it's okay for Joe to be a hero in the Ardennes, but not a crazy Jew in the United States?"—which got me zilch with my relatives, bent on assimilating into the dominantly Protestant United States after World War II. You see, our family's litmus test, first and foremost, was: "Is it good for the Jews?" When Hank Greenberg had the most runs batted in, or Dolph Schayes won another game for Syracuse, or President Harry S. Truman recognized the State of Israel; asking the rhetorical question felt good, because we knew the answer gave us honor. Felix Frankfurter, and Jonas Salk, were good for the Jews, Father Coughlin, and Adolph Hitler, were not. "Bugsy"

Seigel, and Meyer Lansky, were, well... like my cousin, Joe. In all fairness, I haven't seen Mel Brooks' "masterpiece," but reading the ecstatic reviews for *The Producers* made me think of my Aunt Florence. I wonder what she would have felt about the show's central character, a devious Jewish producer, and his scheme to raise double the amount of money necessary (albeit from little old ladies' savings), in order to produce a flop show, after which the investors are told the show's cost was a total loss, leaving him with twice his pound of flesh. Funny? Yes. Good for the Jews? No.

3

MEREDITH WILLSON

THE MUSIC MAN
THE UNSINKABLE MOLLY BROWN
HERE'S LOVE

You could say my journey towards *The Music Man* began in 1951 when I haunted the NBC radio studios in Rockefeller Center, especially Studio 8H where Toscanini conducted the NBC Symphony, and where Meredith Willson conducted the orchestra and chorus for *The Big Show*, starring Tallulah Bankhead. I was 19 then; a clarinetist, vocal arranger and conductor—cocksure of being the next Fred Waring—having appeared with my chorus on NBC and CBS television's, *Prize Performance, Songs For Sale, Horn and Hardart Hour*, and *Wendy Barrie*. The novelty of an adolescent conductor was wearing thin, however, when fate sounded it's French horn and I was drafted. Remembering Meredith Willson was the head of Armed Forces Radio Service during World War II, I crashed Studio 8H, found Willson, and asked if he would recommend me for AFRS. He asked to see my vocal arrangements, and miraculously, liked them. Meredith's specialty at the time was "The Talking Men" a speaksong male chorus that spoke rhythmically (the device was to become famous when Willson wrote "Rock Island," the opening number for *The Music Man*), so not only did Willson give me the recommendation, he also put me to work writing vocal arrangements for his chorus.

Three years later after serving in the USAF, meeting Frank Loesser and joining his music publishing company, I was promoted to governor-general of Frank Music's West coast office and contacted Willson who was living in West Los Angeles. As always, he was gracious and generous and asked if I would like to listen to his new musical, *The Silver Triangle*, which Feuer and Martin had recently dropped. It was the second time my relationship with a songwriter was to change my life. The musical was retitled *The Music Man*, Frank Music Corp. became the publisher, I was assigned to work on the score exclusively, and my journey took wings, or in this case, took tracks. In his book *But He Doesn't Know the Territory*, a diary of how

The Music Man made it to Broadway, Willson wrote:

Next day Herb says, "Mere, I got some good news. Our top man for records is Stu Ostrow. Says he knows you. He'd be the greatest man to handle *Music Man*. We've got a couple other new scores coming in and, of course, *Happy Fella* and *Kismet* are still hot but Stu wants to go exclusively on *Music Man*." A score three record companies turned down, yet.

"Stu Ostrow?" I says. Sure. I remembered Stu Ostrow. Just a young guy. Back in '50 he came over to talk to me about Armed Forces Radio, my alma mater during the war. He was about to go into the Air Force to pay the government a couple years he owed them and hoped I could give him a recommendation to somebody in charge of the Entertainment part of the outfit, so he could keep progressing in music activity and theatre and like that if possible. I remember sending him to some colonel and getting a very nice telegram back from Stu thanking me. You often get requests like that but you don't often get thank-you telegrams back. Sure I remember Stu Ostrow and his telegram. I reproduce it here for a reason that will be clear to you later.

DEC 1951

DEAR MR. WILLSON THANK YOU FOR BEING SO KIND

I SHALL NOT SOON FORGET IT, RESPECTFULLY

STUART OSTROW. A/1C USAF

Then on opening night out-of-town in Philadelphia: Rini and I got in bed with our opening-night wires I had been carrying around since eight o'clock. The first one was from Stu Ostrow, my young friend of years ago, now at Frank Music who at his own request was going to be in charge of *Music Man* for record albums. I was thrown for a moment when I read an odd date down in the body of the message:

Nov. 18, 1957   N.Y. TO PHILA. PA.   4: 23 P.M.

DEC 1951

DEAR MR. WILLSON THANK YOU FOR BEING SO KIND.

I SHALL NOT SOON FORGET IT. RESPECTFULLY

STUART OSTROW. A/1C USAF

(He didn't forget, either. Besides the original cast album, twenty-one separate album interpretations have been recorded to date.)"

From the opening speak-song in the "Rock Island" railway coach for traveling salesmen, to the River City High School assembly hall finale where con man Harold Hill's promised "think system" is realized, Broadway audiences were entranced by Meredith Willson's valentine to 1912 Iowa and his lovable River City (read Mason City) characters. When Willson, fresh from Mason City, Iowa, first came to Chicago as a piccolo player in John Philip Sousa's 1924 famous marching band and was handed a plate of a dozen oysters at a welcoming cocktail party, he didn't know what to make of them. Thirty minutes later when the hostess returned and noticed only one of the succulent oysters had been eaten, asked: "Mr. Willson, don't you care for our big city oysters?" Meredith managed a crooked smile, and pointing to his puckered-clenched teeth, replied in muffled syllables: " I 'ont 'eden 'ike 'is 'un." Three decades later, no longer a rube, he paid homage to The March King by writing this introduction to "Seventy-Six Trombones," for Harold Hill in *The Music Man.*

HAROLD HILL

And you'll see the glitter of crashing cymbals, And you'll hear the thunder of rolling drums, the shimmer of trumpets—Tantara! And you'll feel something akin to the electric thrill I once enjoyed when Gilmore, Liberatti, Pat Conway, The Great Creatore, W.C. Handy and John Philip Sousa, all came to town of the very same historic day!

Then in a brisk 6/8-march tempo, announced by five drum ruffles and a blast of brass (BA-BA-BA-BA-BAA-BA-BA-BA-BOOM! BOOM! BOOM!), Harold parades a thousand reeds, copper bottom timpani, double bell euphoniums, fifty mounted canon, and clarinets of every size into our imaginations. It tore the roof off the Majestic Theatre and if you didn't get up and march at the climax of this number you were either crippled or deaf. Willson also wrote the word "Slam" to denote a rhythmic pause in his speak-songs. "Ya Got Trouble," for example, could be considered the progenitor of today's Rap and Hip-Hop. I recall *The Music Man* gypsy run-through—Broadway jargon for a private performance of a new musical attended by the cast members' family and friends on the last day of rehearsals before the out of town tryout. It was Robert Preston's first musical and he was struggling to read a revised lyric Willson had written the night before for "Ya Got Trouble." Everyone thought "Pres" would choke in front of his first, albeit friendly, audience, but instead he finished the song by throwing the sheet music in the air without missing a Slam.

Meredith Willson was a consummate musician, pianist, composer, lyricist, conductor, and performer. He could write marches, barbershop quartets, speak-songs, ballads, and occasionally an aria, such as "My White Knight," or a love song for a beguiled librarian who never heard bells ringing or saw birds winging, "Till There Was You." Loesser affectionately called "Till There Was You" Meredith's deaf, dumb, and blind song. One of my fondest memories of Meredith was watching him at a backer's audition performing "Gary Indiana." It was a soft-shoe charm song he wrote for a lisping child that "hardly hath any etheth in it," and after Willson was done hissing each *etheth* word, there wasn't a dry angel within spritzing distance from the piano.

In a sense *The Music Man* is also a love story about a husband and a wife—Rini and Meredith—a little half-French, half Russian girl who grew up to marry a piccolo player from Mason City, Iowa, and how together they lived through the events leading up to watching their only child, a Broadway musical comedy called *The Music Man*, come out onto the New York Stage in front of God and everybody, make its bow and speak its piece.

An unintelligible Tammy Grimes, and inexperienced theatre director, Dore Schary, sank Meredith Willson's second Broadway launch, *The Unsinkable Molly Brown*. (Debbie Reynolds' film version of *Molly Brown's* "I Ain't Down Yet" redeemed the property.) Meredith was exasperated with Tammy's mumbling song delivery and asked me to sneak Barbara Cook, his Marion from *The Music Man*, to Philadelphia with the hope she would replace "The stinkable Molly Brown." Barbara was gracious but after watching the musical she demurred, telling me she thought Tammy was terrific and urging us to stay the course. (My hunch was she didn't like the show or the part.) I also recall Willson's meeting with aging producer Lawrence Langner of The Theatre Guild; the author and director didn't get along, and Langner lectured Schary and Willson for twenty minutes on the necessity of "listening to each other." After he finished, Meredith articulated his grievances and turned to Langner for solace, only to find him asleep. It was another dramatization of the malaise that would soon erode the Broadway corpus.

Meredith Willson's adaptation of the classic film, *Miracle On 34th Street*, re-entitled, *Here's Love*, was my first solo production to reach Broadway. Rehearsals weren't going well—author/director problems—so at Meredith's urging I replaced Norman Jewison as director and with the help of Michael Kidd's dances and musical staging the show was a soft hit. (It recouped its investment.)

Television star Craig Stevens (*Peter Gunn*) and Janis Paige were understandably insecure at having a novice director so I wasn't surprised when after asking Craig to exit at a certain point he asked: "How many steps should I take?" Or when Janis asked for an entirely new wardrobe during the premiere tryout in Detroit. Comics Fred Gwynne and David Doyle were more tolerant; even I couldn't kill their laughs. Gwynne (who became one of our great character actors) with true show business grit returned to open the show after the tragic drowning of his baby daughter during rehearsals.

My fondest memory of the musical was the encouragement I received from the gypsy chorus of *Here's Love*. Fixing the show out of town was like a trip to the dentist; so when after another grueling session with the stars a particularly talented dancer who had watched every rehearsal told me "It's getting better," I believed him. His name was Michael Bennett. Our smash opening in Washington, D.C. helped boost morale and allowed the cast and crew a hot August afternoon off to attend Martin Luther King Jr.'s Freedom March and hear the inspiring "I Have a Dream" speech. The perks of being a pre-Broadway hit were numerous but none more special than having Evelyn Lincoln, President Kennedy's secretary, escort my wife around the Oval Office (Ann got to sit in JFK's rocking chair) in return for two house seats to the National Theatre.

In the sixties American Presidents attended the theatre regularly. John F. Kennedy in 1961 had the Forty-Sixth Street Theatre audience on it's feet when he walked down the aisle to his seat for *How to Succeed in Business Without Really Trying.* So when Harry S. Truman and Richard M. Nixon attended *Here's Love* on the same evening at the Sam S. Shubert Theatre the actors had a tough time keeping the audience's attention towards the stage. As was the custom after the final curtain, both the former President and Vice President were

invited backstage to meet the cast, but when Truman discovered Nixon had tipped off the press during intermission to send photographers, he balked at being camera-friendly with Tricky Dick. Understandable, given his often quoted opinion "Richard Nixon is a no good, lying bastard."

The last scene in the musical took place in Macy's window and was the backdrop for celebrities to be photographed. Truman would have none of it and told us the only way he would pose with Nixon backstage was to have Santa Claus appear at his side and the stars (Janis Paige and Craig Stevens) in-between himself and the Republican cloth coat candidate. The Paparazzi got the historic shot and when it was over Nixon tried to chat up the President. I recall his saying something like: "Mr. President, I hope one day to visit a Broadway show as President of the United States, just as you have today." To which Harry S. Truman, referring to the set, replied: "Dick, if that day ever comes, I'll kiss your ass in Macy's window." When in 1970, Nixon was in the White House and I invited Mr. Truman to attend a performance of *1776* he responded: "To my regret, a heavy load of 'homework' will keep me at my desk for some months to come." My hunch is the real reason he never attended another Broadway show was the specter of Richard Milhous Nixon's behind.

4

JERRY BOCK AND SHELDON HARNICK

FIORELLO!
SHE LOVES ME
FIDDLER ON THE ROOF
THE APPLE TREE

Rodgers and Hammerstein's *The Sound of Music* opened the week before Jerry Bock and Sheldon Harnick's *Fiorello!* In a mere seven days, two decades of collaboration ended for one team of writers, and for the other, two decades were about to begin. Jerry and Sheldon started as special material writers, which simply meant they were funny. Bock wrote sketches for the Camp Tamiment summer shows and music for Sid Caesar's and Max Leibman's television show, *Admiral Broadway Revue*, while Harnick was contributing material to revues: *Two's Company, New Faces of 1952,* and John Murray Anderson's *Almanac.* Bock wrote the score (with Larry Holofcener and George David Weiss) for *Mr. Wonderful* that produced a terrific song, "Too Close for Comfort." Harnick's "The Shape of Things," from *The Littlest Revue* was an early example of his wit, erudition, and felicity of phrase. *The Body Beautiful* was Bock and Harnick's first Broadway show, but it all came together with *Fiorello!*

Fiorello! had the exuberance and moxie of its title character, Fiorello LaGuardia, Great Depression–era mayor of the city of New York, including the exclamation point. H. L. Mencken wrote: "Politicians as a class radiate a powerful odor. What really concerns them first, last, and all the time is simply their own jobs." Bock and Harnick's "Politics And Poker" cooked up the source of that odor, revealing a ward heeler's poker game criteria for selecting a congressman. Jerry Bock set the lyric in waltz tempo to underscore the frivolity of their cynicism. Another waltz, "Till Tomorrow" is more romantic and as with "Tonight" uses Shakespeare's *Romeo and Juliet* as inspiration. In "Little Tin Box," a textbook comedy/character song, Harnick's knowing lyrics give the crooked New York City politicians a lovable point of view while Bock soft-shoes the rogues and charlatans into a time step. The politicians are still tap dancing today. *Fiorello!* won the Pulitzer Prize that year and I

remember promising myself one day I would work with Bock and Harnick.

She Loves Me was a jewel-box of a musical, filled with precious songs and dazzling performances. Joe Masteroff, Bock, and Harnick were on to something new for Broadway—literate, romantic, and without big production numbers: an intimate musical. The choreographer's billing: Music *Number* Staged by Carol Haney, testified to how little a dance enthusiast could expect. William and Jean Eckart's design was masterful and conjured up the elegance of a tasteful, Austro-Hungarian specialty shop. (Only the device for the passing of seasons—icicles suddenly appearing above Maraczek's window—jarred.) Barbara Cook's "Ice Cream" was a moment I save for a rainy day and Jack Cassidy found his most memorable career role as Mr. Kadoly, the villain you can't help but love.

We know of many examples of the Soliloquy Song, in which a character alone on stage confesses and questions his/her thoughts and feelings, and none is more poignant than "Will He Like Me?" Something bruised inside of Sheldon Harnick enabled him to express Amalia Balash's feelings of insecurity and desperation when she is faced with meeting her "Dear Friend," who until now has been a writing correspondent. "Days Gone By" was more than nostalgia. Bock and Harnick transform Maraczek into his younger self as he tentatively remembers a melody and some girl who happened to catch his eye, then re-enacts the waltz-steps of his life. Touching. Auditioning for a sales position in Maraczek's store, Amalia's talent becomes evident when she convinces a chocolate junkie ("No More Candy") that the shop's music box is her salvation. Georg, the "Dear Friend," is equally nervous and upset at the prospect of meeting his unknown pen pal and the writers give him a torrent of thoughts in one breath. "Tonight at Eight" requires a singer with world-class

lungs. The title song "She Loves Me" has the syncopated musical drive of a Count Basie Band, including an eleven-beat "Johnny One Note" build at the end of its bridge to galvanize the last chorus, plus the exuberant lyricism of Georg's unguarded feelings now that he knows the lady in question is Amalia.

"Too Jewish," said William Paley, Chairman of the Board of CBS, and also a Jew; so after years of similar rejections, the original producer of *Fiddler on the Roof*, Fred Coe, was compelled to sell the rights to Harold Prince who ultimately delivered it to Broadway. Jerome Robbins told me it was the memory of his father that inspired him and the great director nurtured the creative process by constantly insisting the writers answer a crucial dramatic question: "What is it about?" Finally the answer came; Tradition. (I was to experience Mr. Robbins' trenchant query first hand when we worked on *The Apple Tree.*) Wisdom is rare so when it surfaces in a Broadway musical it is indeed a cause for celebration. *Fiddler on the Roof* is the case in point. Here was the music from the God of Abraham and Isaac, accessible to all religions.

Talking to God ("If I Were a Rich Man"), Tevye muses although it's no disgrace being poor, it's no great honor either. Bock and Harnick then take the bold step of writing an authentic Yiddish chant as a lilting refrain, ignoring the Broadway establishment naysayers advice not to be "too Jewish." The writers understood the desire to be rich is universal, whether it's implored by a poor milkman in Anatevka, Russia, or a Lotto player in Anaheim, California. In "Matchmaker," Yente, who schemes to bring about a marriage in an old country 1905 shtetl, has the same assignment as another turn of the century matchmaker, Dolly, from Yonkers. (Coincidentally, *Dolly* and *Fiddler* both opened on Broadway in 1964 across the street from each other.) Tevye's three unmarried

daughters, imagining Yente telling them she's found them a match, gaily mimic her pragmatism, but their bravado self-ridicule turns halting restraint for the final chorus when they admit they're terrified! In this brief moment Bock and Harnick demonstrate Tzeitel, Hodel, and Chava's vulnerability and enlighten us regarding nineteenth-century marriage traditions.

In a more contemplative waltz, Bock and Harnick's ceremonial prayer for "Sunrise, Sunset" cries out to parents of the bride and groom throughout the world. "Miracle of Miracles" was somehow overshadowed by the rest of this landmark score, possibly due to its being performed by a comic character, but miraculous nevertheless. With Old Testament references a timid tailor celebrates his marriage to the woman of his dreams. Having a sagacious comedy number ("Do You Love Me?") in the second act of a musical is valuable because it provides welcome relief from the plot. Rarely does it dramatize character, as it does for Tevye and Golde when after twenty-five of marriage they suppose they love each other. Is it any wonder *Fiddler on the Roof* is performed in a dozen countries worldwide? You don't have to be Jewish to take love for granted. Zero Mostel was brilliant as Tevye, the milkman, but he became so unpredictable—ad libbing lines and screaming at the other actors—that Prince didn't renew his contract. Hal was right and *Fiddler on the Roof* proved to be more than a Zero.

After writing *Fiddler on the Roof,* Jerry Bock and Sheldon Harnick were studying the short story form as the basis for their next musical when I called and asked if they would be interested in creating an evening of three musicals connected to a common theme. Coincidence? I think not. Theatre never invents new ideas, it acts in response to what is already in the air, and my assumption was television had reduced the audience's attention span to half hour program-

ming so why not dramatize one acts on stage without commercial interruption? We began immediately.

The joy of creating a new work is in its research and it was a revelation reading the short stories of Boccaccio, Chekhov, Dickens, de Maupassant, Hawthorne, Poe, Gogol, and Zola, as well as investigating the treasury of novella writers, such as Frank O'Connor, Hemingway, Joyce, Faulkner, D. H. Lawrence, Katherine Mansfield and Katherine Ann Porter, the Argentine Borges, Donald Barthelme, and Nelson Algren. We learned the best part about using the short story as source material is you didn't have to worry about second act problems. What challenged us however was to find three stories that would coalesce into a theatrical unity.

Our original title was *Come Back, Go Away, I Love You* and we chose Bruce Jay Friedman's short story "Show Biz Connections" as the first to be musicalized, the *Come Back* part. It was a bawdy, black humor romance concerning a shambling, ugly loser who makes a pact with the devil to show up in the last desperate moments of a beautiful woman's life in order to have sex. They copulate, she dies, but he survives to fiddle again—until he falls in love with number 32—only to exchange places with her as she escapes with the devil, leaving him to die. "The Lady or The Tiger," Frank Stockton's much admired puzzle, is a story of a youth so bold as to love the King's daughter and who is condemned to open one of two doors. Behind one is a fascinating girl whom he must marry; behind the other is a tiger. The King's daughter learns the secret and signals her lover to open one of the two doors, but which? (The *Go Away* part.) The last story was "The Diary Of Adam And Eve," a delightful sampling of the timeless wit and fertile imagination of Mark Twain, who pictures the first couple as they find themselves trapped in paradise. *I Love You*, of course.

The notion was to find three tales that would exemplify each entreaty, with all to be performed by the same cast. Our theory was there would be a cumulative outcome for the leading characters, having lived distinctly different lives somehow symbolically connected. Piece of cake. Enter director Jerome Robbins. "What is it about?" he asked. *Oy vey.* For the next fifteen months of meetings, casting, rehearsals, out-of-town tryouts, and opening on Broadway, we tried but never did answer the question. Robbins was patient but remained uncommitted to the project for nearly a year and Sheldon, Jerry and I were experiencing *shpilkes* (the jumps) so I approached Mike Nichols to direct. He had awards up the wazoo for *Barefoot in the Park, The Odd Couple,* and *Luv,* all comedies, and since our evening had a lot of laughs we thought he would respond favorably to the material.

Nichols invited us to his fashionable Hollywood digs to audition the show but what we didn't know was he had also invited all his celebrity friends to be our audience. Julie Andrews, Blake Edwards, Andre Previn, Mia Farrow—and a dozen other alter egos—there to tell Mike what he thought. *Nichols didn't have a clue about how to direct a musical.* It was a warning I blithely ignored because he was bankable and I was ambitious. "I'll do it if you drop the Bruce Jay Friedman story," Mike told me the next morning. I was stunned since "Show Biz Connections" was a knockout at the audition and when I reported his terms to direct back to the team, Sheldon Harnick literally threw up all over the Beverly Hills Hotel, then caught the next flight out of LA to New York. (I later learned Bruce Jay Friedman had turned down writing a screenplay for Mike and refusing Nichols can be hairy, so to speak.) Jerry Bock was thoughtful and, as is his custom, he only saw the positive side. "What story does he suggest we substitute?" Bock asked, and when we visited

Mike that afternoon (sans Harnick) our new director suggested Jules Feiffer's "Passionella." Furthermore, Mike wanted to begin the evening with *The Diary of Adam and Eve* and call the show *The Apple Tree.* There's always a defining moment in the life of a musical. If you forget what excited you about the show in the first light of its creation and accept another concept, the result will be muddled. Welcome to *I don't know what the show is about.*

Sheldon and Jerry wrote a cartoon score for the *Village Voice* illustrator's "Passionella" and we began to cast. The directors mission is to insulate themselves from the vicissitudes of showbiz so they always hire a cast that will make them look good. With Fosse, it was dancers first. As for Nichols—a former standup comic with Elaine May—it was funny people. Mike adored Barbara Harris. They had worked together in Paul Sills' *Second City* improvisational group in Chicago and notwithstanding her limited vocal range we hired her without an audition.

Finding a leading man who was both musical and hilarious was tough and we hit bottom when Michael Shurtleff, our genius-casting director, brought a monosyllabic, whispering, ill at ease actor to audition as Adam. "What are you going to sing?" I asked. "I don't sing," Dustin Hoffman replied. "I'm Zoditch in *The Journey of the Fifth Horse,*" referring to Ronald Ribman's new play at the American Place Theatre in St. Clements's Church. "Then why are you here?" Nichols hissed, in his signature-chic-ridicule-delivery. I sensed Dustin was intimidated so I suggested he sing "Happy Birthday," a failsafe song for nonsingers. "How does it go?" Hoffman asked straight-faced. He wasn't kidding, and after the accompanist played the tune a dozen times for Dustin Hoffman, he auditioned and bombed. (Mike Nichols' next project, however, was the film *The Graduate* and he didn't forget Dustin.)

We tried casting Al Freeman Jr., an African-American as Adam, but this was 1966, the year of Black Power and White Backlash, and Broadway, then as now, was lily-white. It was Alan Alda's audition of "If I Only Had a Brain" which won him the role and a headache for me when he broke his contract to star in a television series.

The first song Jerry and Sheldon wrote for "The Diary of Adam and Eve" portion of the evening was "Beautiful, Beautiful World," an opening number expressing Eve's first awareness of the beauty around her. It was a diversified, curious, fascinating, bountiful, beautiful, beautiful song and when during rehearsals it became obvious Barbara Harris couldn't sing it we all felt prematurely expelled from the Garden of Eden. God created heaven and earth in six days. It took Bock and Harnick five days to create a replacement opening number, "Here In Eden," another miracle, albeit a professional one. Everything happens for the best. Writing the world's first love song for Adam to sing about Eve is as difficult as trying to bottle a kiss. Nevertheless the writers met the dramatic challenge by having Adam at first irritated with Eve and in the release changing the mood from a measured drone to a free-wheeling burst of melody and astonished revelation that she is beautiful. "What Makes Me Love Him" in other hands could have resulted in a song wallowing in sentimentality. Not so with the authors of *Fiorello!*, *She Loves Me*, and *Fiddler on the Roof*, who has Eve come to the conclusion that the reason she loves Adam is merely that he's masculine, and hers. After the first twenty-five years of creation it's nice to know.

Tony Walton was our brilliant designer and was overwhelmed having to design both scenery and costumes for three musicals at the same time. During rehearsals I received an emergency call from the scenery shop to look at the set being built for Act One,

"The Diary of Adam and Eve." What I saw was a disaster. Tony had designed an Eden stamped out of plastic molds where everything: the shelter, trees, lakes, and animals, were translucent! It looked like *Star Wars*, not Mark Twain. When I confronted Mike Nichols with the colossal problem of lighting such surfaces, he merely said (in his best Caligula imitation): "It's what I want. If you desire genius, you must pay for it," and threatened to walk. Walton agreed there was a problem but he felt a loyalty to deliver Nichols' vision, so I paid for it— $80,000 of trouble.

When we had our technical rehearsal in Boston, it took Jean Rosenthal four days (unheard of in 1966) to light plastic city, but now we were finally ready to run the show. "Barbara, Alan, on stage!" Nichols called out. "We're here," two disembodied voices replied. *We couldn't see the actors!* Nichols turned pale, then said to me: "Tell Tony it doesn't work; throw it out, we need another set." Walton was inconsolable. He knew the cost of the set was a third of the show's budget, and that like the snake in Eden, I didn't have a pit to hiss in. But it was when I saw Tony sketching under a tree in the Boston Gardens, I was hopeful the new set would be closer to nature. It was: organic, beautiful, and down to earth at $9000.

What do Robert Klein, Jerome Robbins, Herbert Ross and Nora Kaye, Jacqueline Kennedy, Lillian Hellman, Mia Farrow, Gloria Steinem, Penelope Gilliatt, Richard Williams, Alexander Cohen, and Warren Beatty have to do with *The Apple Tree*? Answer: Klein was in the chorus, his first Broadway show, direct from Chicago's *Second City*. Director/Choreographers Herb and Nora commuted from Hollywood to help friend Nichols, who was a terrific comedy director but froze every time the music started. Jerome Robbins, our original director came to our rescue during previews in New York and unified the three stories by having the Narrator wear a tuxedo in each

act. (For the record, he never asked for any payment.) President Kennedy's widow, Hellman, Farrow, Gloria, and Penelope, were Nichols' personal friends who showed up during Hollywood prepro- duction conferences, New York rehearsals, and the Boston tryout. (I nearly swooned when Mrs. Kennedy tapped me on the shoulder and asked how much I was paying the musicians.)

Richard Williams (the genius film animator who later did *Who Framed Roger Rabbit?*) created a stunning five-minute montage for the transformation of Barbara Harris' Ella to Passionella. Warren Beatty was dating Barbara when she was nominated for the Best Actress in a Musical Tony Award, and was scheduled to appear on producer Alex Cohen's first nationally televised Tony Awards pro- gram. The afternoon of the telecast Alex called me and said: "You'd better come to the theatre, Stuart, Barbara doesn't want to come out of her dressing room." When I arrived Barbara addressed me as Nichols: "Mike, Please tell Stuart I'm sorry but I can't go on," and walked out the stage door. I followed her on to a downtown bus, and then to her town house on Fifth Street in Greenwich Village. Her friends tried to help me coax her back uptown, but she was clearly not herself. It wasn't until I called Beatty that I discovered they had just split up. Miraculously he got her to the theatre, through the Awards performance and ceremony (she won the Best Actress Tony Award) and even brought her to the gala party afterward. Where she still called me Mike.

5

SHERMAN EDWARDS AND PETER STONE

1776

At rise. Sherman Edwards was obsessed with the founding fathers. It took him more than a decade to write the book, music and lyrics to the musical and he told me of his many visits to Philadelphia, especially to Benjamin Franklin's gravesite in order to sing Ben his latest draft. I loved Sherman for that. On the occasion of our 1970 opening in London he wrote this dedication in the published book version of *1776*: "To Stuart: in whom I reposed a firm reliance—and affected a joint alliance with divine Providence—Sherm." It was the culmination of a bumpy journey beginning in 1967 when Sherman first played his score for me at 1501 Broadway. Like most songwriters of his time who had to plug their own material he *sold the song;* giving the characters a dimension never equaled by the on-stage actors. As with Berlin, Porter, and Loesser, those giants who wrote and performed both words and music, Edwards owned all the emotional content of the story so when he performed the score you believed he was John Adams. His score was terrific but the book paid excessive homage to the ghosts of Franklin and Jefferson and consequently lacked dramatic tension. Getting Sherman to agree to take on a collaborator was difficult He was almost 50 years old and cited Meredith Willson who was 55 when *The Music Man* opened on Broadway and who also wrote its book, music and lyrics. I told Sherman I was prepared to wait until he was 55, if necessary, if he didn't allow me to try. He agreed, courteously.

I first approached William F. Buckley Jr., the prolific editor for the *National Review* to come on-board as a co–book writer. After all he was a patriot, albeit an infuriating one, and I thought he might relish the challenge of writing for the stage. He declined; the first in a long line of writers, Arthur Laurents was another, who didn't think the idea of a musical about the Declaration of Independence was a revolutionary concept. (Buckley wrote a gracious congratulatory note

after seeing *1776*, and Laurents, at intermission during previews told me he "admired my perseverance.") Then there was Peter Stone. He had written a witty, revisionist book for *Kean,* about the celebrated 19th century English actor, a near-hit of a musical, and what *1776* needed most was irreverence in its historical characterizations to match the lighthearted, Gilbert & Sullivan-ish, impertinence of Sherman's score.

It was essential that the stodgy American icons as depicted in our history books were dramatized as human, fallible men. Of course that was the secret of the show's success. Audiences giggled at Thomas Jefferson giving the Continental Congress weather report while lusting to return home having not seen his wife for six months, and were delighted when the epigrammatic Benjamin Franklin was put down in this exchange with John Dickinson, also of Pennsylvania:

Dickinson (pounding the desk):

No, sir! *Englishmen!!*

Franklin (he's been asleep, his chin on his chest; now an eye opens):
Please, Mr. Dickinson—but must you start banging? How is a man to sleep?

Laughter.

Dickinson:

Forgive me, Dr. Franklin, but must you start speaking? How is a man to stay awake?

Laughter.

We'll promise to be quiet, sir. I'm sure everyone prefers that you remain asleep.

Franklin:

If I'm to hear myself called an Englishman, sir, then I assure you I'd prefer I'd remain asleep.

Dickinson:

What's so terrible about being called an Englishman? The English don't seem to mind.

Franklin:

Nor would I, given the full rights of an Englishman. But to call me one *without* those rights is like calling an ox a bull—he's thankful for the honor but he'd much rather have restored what's rightfully his.

Laughter, Franklin laughing the longest.

Dickinson (finally):

When did you first notice they were missing, sir?

Laughter.

Neither Dumas Malone nor Samuel Eliot Morrison could ever have written that because the Congress secretary Charles Thompson kept no minutes of the 1776 debates, recording only those motions that were passed. Tainted history? Perhaps, but pure theatre.

As a strong advocate of author's rights Stone became president of The Dramatists Guild (1985–1999) and didn't trust producers, especially one who was continually shooting arrows into the air, hoping that they might fall somewhere that counted. I recall nipping at his heels regarding John Dickinson, the ostensible villain of *1776*, as being too easy a target, a paper tiger. One afternoon during rehearsals when I suggested a line change in the "Ox/Bull" debate it was greeted with Peter's shrill reprimand, in the presence of the cast, something to the effect that no one writes lines except the *author* and that was Peter Stone! Everyone was stunned so I immediately asked Peter into another room and reminded him I was Frank Loesser–trained that a producer is someone who knows a writer and of course I wouldn't change a line without his consent. Perhaps it was what I said, or his embarrassment at having blownup, but Peter Stone

and I valued each other from that moment on. Earlier negotiations then with Peter were as fractious as those between the Israelis and Palestinians today, especially when it came to billing. Peter wanted sole book writer credit and Sherman continued evoking Meredith Willson's *Music Man* billing. We were at an impasse until I remembered Franklin Lacey. Lacey had helped Meredith with his original story (called *The Silver Triangle* before it became *The Music Man*) and that at the eleventh hour Meredith told me to add the following to his billing: *Based on a story by* MEREDITH WILLSON and FRANKLIN LACEY. Armed with that esoteric evidence I was able to propose a compromise, which both parties grudgingly accepted:

STUART OSTROW *Presents*

1776

Music and Lyrics by **SHERMAN EDWARDS**
Book by **PETER STONE**

Based on a conception of Sherman Edwards

Peter considered *1776* his best work (deservedly so) so one may forgive him for insisting on the revised billing: "A Musical Play by Peter Stone and Sherman Edwards," for the cover of The Viking Press publication. Retribution. Curiously, they seldom collaborated. Peter wrote several drafts of the new book with new cues for the songs and one day handed us the rebirth of Sherman's concept all grown up; intelligent, touching, funny and what's more, believable. It was a feat of playwriting craft I've seldom seen equaled in another musical.

Now all I had to do was raise $350,000, find a director, try to book a Broadway theatre, and cast a show that everyone believed was doomed to failure. Well, not everyone. Jerome Robbins was my theatre conscience ever since we worked together on *We Take the Town*,

The Apple Tree, and *A Pray by Blecht.* He insisted on quality. Which meant investment of the best skill and effort possible to produce the finest and most admirable result possible. So, of course, I asked him to direct *1776.* By 1969 he had quit Broadway, in favor of creating dances for the New York City Ballet, but he thought the show was exceptional and encouraged me to hire a young, unknown director, Peter Hunt. Wow, I thought, I didn't get Robbins but he liked the show! There was never a more defining moment for *1776,* one that I kept in mind when each new disaster struck. Neither Stone nor Edwards were thrilled with the prospect of hiring Hunt, a Yale lighting designer cum-director, whose only credit was a Lincoln Center production of the play *Booth,* about the notorious assassin. After all this was Broadway, the big leagues, and you didn't gamble with unknowns. "At least he likes historical characters," I kidded on the square. No one laughed so I went to work recruiting other directors.

Finding the best writer for *1776* was hard but this new quest would have discouraged Don Quixote. Starting with the *As*: George Abbott, William Ball, Gower Champion, Morton Da Costa, Alvin Epstein, Bob Fosse, and Andre Gregory all turned me down and nearly a quarter-way through the alphabet it struck me I might have better luck with an English director. Since historically the Brits squandered the revolution, my pitch would be: "*1776* will repay England for the loss of her Colonies." I contacted Peter Hall at the RSC and surprise he loved it! H̲ was our lucky letter. Hall and I exchanged possible rehearsal and out-of-town tryout dates and for a few blissful few months I began raising the capitalization for the production.

It was my good fortune to have Edgar M. Bronfman as my partner and after listening to my plans for the production and a demo of the score he asked: "How much and how soon?" I was

speechless but then mistakenly opened my mouth and, almost fatally, inquired: "Don't you want to read the book?" Edgar looked a *hole* through me and said: "Nooo...that's why you're my partner. Is there something wrong with it?" *Never open a closed deal,* I shuddered to myself, but mercifully Edgar let it pass. (I was to repeat this stupidity in 1980 when Edgar asked me how much money I needed to bring the musical *Swing,* running in Washington to Broadway, but this time he let *Swing* pass away.) Edgar brought another partner into *1776,* Bill Green, who was late with his investment because he "had to wait until his bank CD matured." Edgar advanced his share. A mysterious man, Green entertained lavishly, trying to vie with Bronfman's life style by building a lavish home in Mt. Kisco, and was one giant pain in the ass. He nearly scuttled a million dollar deal with Jack Warner to buy the motion picture rights because he wanted to be a movie producer. "Producing is bullshit, Stu," he declared, "you're just a businessman, like me, only you got a Tony Award. Let's buy the rights and do it ourselves."

When I went to the famed movie legend and Pound Ridge, New York neighbor Joe Mankiewicz for advice he said Green was Jay Gatsby and to sell *1776* to Jack Warner. Sage advice. Ever since the Warner Bros. movie opened at Radio City Music Hall in 1972, it is played on television stations nationwide every Fourth of July. Back to 1968. We now had a resurrected book, $350,000, and Peter Hall. All we needed was a Broadway theatre so I made an appointment to see Lawrence Shubert Lawrence, the last scion of the Shubert line, who was a friend and admired my productions of *Here's Love* and *The Apple Tree,* both having played the flagship Shubert Theatre.

Before going to Lawrence's office I remember stopping at Sardi's across the street to check my office messages and hearing my secretary say Peter Hall had just "rung in" from London. Since it was

a pay phone booth I had to ask the restaurant cashier for twenty dollars in quarters and proceeded to struggle with AT&T and the English telephone operators. It took twenty minutes and $10.75 to make the connection and when finally Hall was on the line, in-between static, and the ocean's roar I heard something like: "I'm so sorry . . .r boy, but I'm not..ble to direct *1776*, beca. . . . . . RSC has resched. . . .*The Battle of . . ..vings* and. . . ." Suddenly the operator interrupted: "I'm sorry sir, that'll be $10.75 for the next five minutes." "Operator," I screamed, " I only have $9.25 left! Don't cut me off and I'll run downstairs for the 50 cents." "You'll have to replace the call sir," and click, she was gone, London was gone, Peter Hall was gone, and *1776* was sinking in a maelstrom of mass communication. A disaster, but I immediately summoned up the memory of Jerry Robbins' faith in the show and chose to believe it was fate.

What about Peter Hunt? We were stalled at the H's (surely that was a sign) so I asked Stone to meet with Hunt and find out what Robbins saw in the young director. After three days Stone called me with an enthusiastic report and Peter, Sherman and I met with the cheery man in a duffle coat with horn buttons. It was love at second sight and when we listened to Hunt provide details of his vision for our musical we hired him on the spot. Exhilarated, having declared our independence from the Broadway propensity for playing it safe, we not only found our identity but also continued afterward to take leap after leap in the dark. When we opened Walter Kerr, the *New York Times* Sunday Arts & Leisure critic, wrote this about *1776:* "...if you've got any character of your own you'll go see it instantly, just to keep its independence company....Look what it's up to. It won't budge on that title, which cannot be said to have a box office ring to it." He went on to say that in addition to the title, it has no stars, no chorus, and no intermission. For want of 50 cents, a battle was won. Now for the rest of the war.

Peter Hunt admired the great scenic designer, Jo Mielziner, and urged me to hire him for *1776*. The Broadway establishment thought Mielziner wasn't trendy enough in 1968 (more than enough reason to interest me) and we met at his apartment in the Dakota on 72nd Street. A gentle man and gentleman, Jo astonished me. He had not only read our script but had also completed research of Philadelphia's Independence Hall and presented me his sketches for the set of the Continental Congress's Chamber! No contract existed between us, no money had been paid, yet this veteran of 44 bountiful Broadway years designed *1776* on spec. When I asked him why, he simply smiled and replied: "Because it's going to be a hit." Another sign. I promised myself to one day tell about Jo's humble audition as well as this story. The authors had imagined the *1776* finale to be a scrim bleed through from the stage actors signing of the Declaration, to the famous Pine-Savage engraving of the original members of the Continental Congress. It didn't work and I recall Peter Hunt, Jo, and I having breakfast the day after opening at the National Theatre in Washington, DC bemoaning our failure. It was Hunt who suggested we replace the engraving with a copy of the Declaration but it was Mielziner who came up with the visual concept of cropping the document and enlarging the members signatures to conform exactly to where the actors are last seen on stage. He had designed a moment of history.

The next gift from the theatre gods was our casting director, Michael Shurtleff. As well as being a playwright (*Call Me by My Rightful Name*) Michael was resourceful, hard working, and caring concerning the actors he recommended. He always gave me the feeling he was personally involved in the actor's life, similar to a doting parent who proudly details his progeny's talents and insecurities. Michael was the most influential voice in the selection of the *1776*

cast because he'd seen everything the auditioning actors had done and could more accurately envisage their range, intensity, and creativity as a stage persona. Michael had a process, which never varied; that was to parade a succession of candidates until we were bored and then bring his choice on stage at the eleventh hour. I'm certain he had the entire show cast before we ever saw one actor. The one exception was Louise Lasser, a kooky actress who went *Bananas* with Woody Allen and who was recommended by Peter Stone. It was called *protecting the jokes*. We mistakenly cast her as Martha Jefferson and had to replace her during rehearsals. The mistake we made was hiring a comedienne to pump-up the comedy scene in Thomas Jefferson's celibate room in Philadelphia, overlooking the essential fact that Martha had one of the best songs in the show, "He Plays the Violin," a doubled-enten-dre paean to Tom's ability as a lover. So when an unknown Betty Buckley, looking like a cheerleader and straight off the plane from Texas, began her audition by saying: "Howdy!," I thought we had hit bottom. "You're very pretty, Miss Buckley, but not the type, thank you very much," I said. "Won't y'all least hear me sing?" replied the future Grizabella and before I could say no she was into "Johnny One Note," and wiped us out. After her thrilling performance I turned to Peter Stone and Sherman Edwards and asked: "If you were Thomas Jefferson and hadn't seen your wife for six months, would-n't you finish writing the Declaration of Independence the minute Betty Buckley walked in the door?" That is exactly how Peter wrote the scene.

Howard Da Silva, as my haberdasher father said about a hag-gling customer, *was a tough man to shave*. His presence as Ben Franklin was formidable, encouraging the cast to stretch their acting talents and thereby raising the level of the ensemble playing. But he was an old hand in the theatre, not easily directed by a newcomer or pro-

duced by someone with only two Broadway credits, so he challenged every change in the script. Howard sulked for days after Stone gave Dickinson the: "When did you first notice they were missing?" topper, but nothing compared to his rage during our New Haven try-out decision to cut his solo production number, "Doozy Lamb." It was set in New Brunswick, the Continental Army Training Ground, where John Adams, Samuel Chase and Franklin had been deputized as a War Committee to inspect the alleged whoring and the drinking of the American recruits. Neither the scene nor the song belonged in the show. It demeaned Franklin by exaggerating his licentious character, thereby turning him into a cartoon (a similar criticism Steve Sondheim cautioned me about regarding Thomas Jefferson, which we rectified in Washington D.C.) but equally important, it took us away from Mielziner's memorable set and the debate. Howard quit cold when I cut Franklin's vulgar frolic, sung in a New Jersey whorehouse, but returned when his friend Alfred Drake reported seeing his understudy, Rex Everhart, get even more laughs without the scene and song.

As with each decision we made to pare down *1776*, especially confining most events to the chamber of the Continental Congress, the musical improved; but the crucial event occurred on February 8th 1969, my 37th birthday, when fate intervened yet again by providing the Blizzard of '69 in New Haven, Connecticut, the opening night of our out-of-town tryout. Mercifully no one showed up and the public didn't read our terrible reviews the next day—no newspaper deliveries, performances were cancelled, the streets were impassable—but most significantly the creative team was sequestered in the same hotel with no investors, agents, wives, or wiseguys from New York to tell us what was wrong with *1776*. (Ann Ostrow couldn't navigate the frozen highways back to Pound Ridge and, astute in

the ways of theatre, voluntarily sat in the lobby during production meetings in the suite.) Stone, Edwards, Hunt and I met hourly to review rewrites. Food, drink, bed sheets and toilet paper were in short supply (Sherman had irritable bowel syndrome and Stone complained Edwards had "fouled every nest in the hotel.") and I often thought we huddled together just to keep warm.

Cutting "Doozy Lamb," presented a monumental problem. It was the big first act closing number, a romp with chorus girls (including the future Ms. Stephen Schwartz) being chased by Franklin on Mielziner's restoration comedy set, replete with staircases and slamming doors. What could take its place? Hours became days and although the snow was melting and performances resumed, we were still frozen solid without a first act closing number. It was then when I suggested cutting the intermission. I went on to say something like: "rather than end the act with another hellzapoppin' number, let's not replace the song, or end the act at all, but keep the audience in their seats and continue the story without interruption. No musical had ever done it before, another reason to leap in the dark, and besides, everyone gets to go home earlier." A deadly silence followed, much like the one when I suggested changing *1776*'s title to *Fireworks!*, until Peter Stone said, "Let's do it," and left. By the next morning Stone had rewritten the order of the songs, invented a new scene in an anteroom off the main Congressional Chamber, which dramatized a successful Franklin and Adams returning from New Brunswick having gotten Maryland to change its vote, and leaving room for Sherman to write a new song for Ben Franklin in the proper setting. Fireworks indeed.

Our second tryout city was Washington D.C. and the National Theatre, where in 1963 *Here's Love* enjoyed a sold out four weeks. I missed Scott Kirkpatrick, the elegant Southern house man-

ager, whose office was a Collyer brothers clutter of old programs and theatre memorabilia and who was a real leader in the 1950s trying to dismantle the hideous Jim Crow policy of Blacks restricted to the balcony in D.C. Now this was 1969 and civil rights had at last come to the nation's capitol. The incongruity was appalling but so was our fudging of Thomas Jefferson's slavery practices, who when asked by the delegate from South Carolina, Edward Rutledge: "… you are a…*practioner*, are you not?" Jefferson replies: "I have already resolved to release my slaves." Of course he did no such thing. On reflection, it was our responsibility to expose the hypocrisies of the time, especially Thomas Jefferson's, but instead we *resolved* to leave it ambiguous.

Richard Coe, the drama critic of the *Washington Post*, gave *1776* a glowing review and suddenly all the Broadway wise guys wanted a piece of us. Since I had gambled opening out-of-town without a commitment for a Broadway theatre (no stars, no chorus line, no name director, no title), offers now poured in and I chose the 46th Street Theatre. Sherman meanwhile had written "The Egg" for the anteroom scene, inspired by Fay Gage's ingenious art work logo of an eaglet emerging from a Union Jack shell holding the thirteen colony American flag in its beak.

Onna White had the daunting task of staging the *1776* musical numbers (how do you choreograph a cast of 27 non-dancers?) and "He Plays the Violin" was no exception. I remember picking Onna up in New Jersey and driving down to Washington after our closing New Haven, in order to fix Betty Buckley's number. The song just lay there, not because Betty Lynn couldn't belt it to the second balcony, she did, but because it needed movement. I had suggested Martha dance with Franklin and Adams. Onna was unconvinced (ergo my offer of a lift to D.C.) but after four hours of being trapped with her producer, and yet another snowstorm, when we

reached her hotel Onna had Martha Jefferson waltzing John Adams and Benjamin Franklin into giddy exhaustion. And *1776* had another showstopper.

The most important contribution a producer can make during an out-of-town tryout is to remind the creators why they were originally excited about their show. Sometimes it works, as with *A Funny Thing Happened on the Way to the Forum*, *M. Butterfly*, and a few others, but they are the exceptions. The majority of misconceived, underwritten, self-delusional pre-Broadway shows sink. Fortunately our musical paralleled the chaotic situation in *1776*, when the discordant members of the Continental Congress at the penultimate moment adopt the resolution on independence and achieve a hushed harmony:

Hancock:

Very well gentlemen.

(He goes to Thompson's desk and picks up the quill.)

We are about to brave the storm in a skiff made of paper, and how it will end, God only knows.

(He signs with a flourish.)

Franklin:

Hancock's right. This paper is our passport to the gallows. But there's no backing out now. If we don't hang together, we shall most assuredly hang separately.

Providentially, Sherman Edwards, Peter Stone, Peter Hunt, Onna White, Jo Mielziner, Patricia Zipprodt, Peter Howard, Eddie Sauter, Elise Bretton and myself did. *Curtain.*

Curtain Call: In 1968 dissent and doubt regarding the war in Vietnam tore at the Republic and the country was evermore shocked by the assassination of Martin Luther King, Jr., and Senator Robert

F. Kennedy, and by violence surrounding the party conventions in Miami and Chicago. The reason I thought that producing *1776* was so timely then was its relevance to the protest to end the war in Vietnam. America was thwarting Vietnam's revolution in much the same way England sought to defeat us in 1776. It was my secret, and ironically, after President Richard M. Nixon invited us to perform at the White House, the nation's right wing conservatives co-opted the musical's revolutionary character. No one ever knew however that at the eleventh hour a tough lady on Nixon's staff called me with a list of songs the White House insisted be cut from the show for the President's guests. She demanded we take out: "Cool, Cool, Conservative Men, "Momma, Look Sharp," and "Molasses to Rum" (The three were: anti-conservative, anti-war, and anti-race hypocrisy, respectively.) I refused and it was William Safire, a former flack for the League of New York Theaters, then a speechwriter for President Nixon, who convinced the White House to have *1776* performed in its entirety. The only other occasion the prestigious East Room was ever so humbled was when Abigail Adams used it to hang out the family laundry. In an effort to declare our independence from the White House, I took out a full-page ad in the *New York Times* supporting the "McGovern Amendment" to end the Vietnam War, causing one of my investors to threaten to sue, then back off when our box office suddenly increased. It also brought this letter from Senator George McGovern:

GEORGE McGOVERN

SOUTH DAKOTA

UNITED STATES SENATE

WASHINGTON, D.C. 20510

June 25, 1970

RECEIVED JUL 1 1970

Dear Mr. Ostrow:

I was extremely pleased to see the advertisement in the *New York Times* on June 22, 1970, which was placed by the producer, director and authors of "1776."

The fact that a single theatrical production has taken the unprecedented action of advertising its position in connection with the Amendment to End the War is particularly moving. The vote on the Amendment will be extremely important to this country as well as to the people of Indochina. You have helped significantly in the effort to speed the end of the War.

I would appreciate your extending my appreciation to Sherman Edwards, Peter Stone, and Peter Hunt.

With every good wish,
Sincerely yours,
George McGovern

But after all the acclaim and awards it was this letter from Groucho Marx that kept us honest:

GROUCHO MARX

April 7, 1970

Mr. Stuart Ostrow

"1776"

46th Street Theatre

New York City, New York

Dear Mr. Ostrow:

Thanks for the lovely telegram. I am working desperately hard boosting shows that are so clean I would be willing to take my Aunt to see. Unfortunately, she happens to be one of the dirtiest women in America.

At any rate, I love the whole show, including the fellow who played Benjamin Franklin, who can fly a kite for my money any time.

Sincerely,

Groucho (Signed)

Groucho Marx

6

BOB DYLAN AND ARCHIBALD MACLEISH

SCRATCH

In the *New York Times* October 5th 2004 review of Bob Dylan's book of recollections *Chronicles: Volume One, So You Thought You Knew Dylan? Hah! By Janet Maslin,* the following excerpt intrigued me: "Part of 'Chronicles' is devoted to Mr. Dylan's efforts to reinvent himself by many different means. He was invited by Archibald MacLeish to collaborate on a play—a play that wound up closing on its third day." I promptly read *Chronicles* and Dylan's version of his experience with *Scratch,* the Archibald MacLeish play I produced at the St. James Theatre thirty-four years ago. I discovered Mr. Dylan had indeed reinvented all the facts, egregiously.

For openers in Chapter Three, *New Morning,* he begins with: "I had just returned to Woodstock from the Midwest—from my father's funeral. There was a letter from Archibald MacLeish waiting for me on the table...Archie's letter said that he'd like to meet with me to discuss the possibility of me composing some songs for a play he was writing...." Baloney. MacLeish never asked Bob Dylan to collaborate on *Scratch.*

In Scott Donaldson's *Archibald MacLeish: An American Life* (Houghton Mifflin, 1992), Donaldson writes: "The idea for the play came from producer Stuart Ostrow, who had just achieved a hit with the musical *1776.* He sounded out two men fifty years apart in age to write the words and music—MacLeish to adapt the story into a playable script and Bob Dylan to supply the songs. When first approached Archie thought the idea preposterous....And he was suspicious of the collaboration Ostrow had in mind."

Dylan nevertheless continues that he and his wife drove "...to where he lived, to meet with him...the poet of night stones and the quick earth... about his new play.... It was fitting that I go see him." Fantasy.

Eager to find new writers for the musical theatre in the

1970s I commissioned Archibald MacLeish and Bob Dylan to write a new musical, *Scratch*. Here's the *Emes*. Bob Dylan whined a couplet at me to quit pushing him one afternoon while working in my Pound Ridge studio; something like, "If it comes it comes, if it won't it won't, if it rhymes it rhymes, if it don't it don't." Too bad it wasn't a finished song for *Scratch*, the ballad musical I was producing for Broadway. My plan was for MacLeish, the Republic's poet laureate, and Dylan, America's balladeer, to dramatize Stephen Vincent Benét's *The Devil and Daniel Webster* and we were into our third month of unproductive meetings. "How's this?" he asked, handing me a verse and chorus scrawled on a foolscap pad. It was illegible. "Sing it to me Bob; I can't read Sanskrit," I replied, trying for a laugh and hoping to get him to use the guitar he brought each week, yet never played. Dylan mumbled something, then picked up his guitar and sang, "Father of Night," with his signature nasal-monotone assurance. Finally, a breakthrough! Dylan had translated MacLeish's draft of a scene with Daniel Webster and his client, Jabez Stone, into a duet; a repentant prayer for Stone and a defiant challenge for Webster. The musical was going to work and the musical theatre would hear a new generation's voice!

During the following weeks he finished several songs, including the opening number for *Scratch*, "New Morning." There were other signs of progress: Dylan agreed to meet with director Peter Hunt and Archibald MacLeish in Conway, Massachusetts and he brought his musical director, Al Kooper, to Pound Ridge to check me out. It was strange enough driving four hours with Bob Dylan to Conway without his saying a word but nothing compared to the seven hours that followed. The MacLeish's home was a charming eighteenth-century saltbox, with a woodshed that boasted vintage-scented oak, pine, and copper beech logs for the fireplace. Into this

harmony of past and perfect I brought America's troubadour and he freaked. Peter Hunt, the MacLeishs, and I spent the afternoon watching Dylan drink the house brandy as quickly as MacLeish could refill his snifter. He never once responded to any question nor joined the conversation regarding the musical's dramatic problems but kept belting the brandy down so by the time we reached Act Two he was asleep. We were dumfounded. It was time to leave and the only impression the celebrated folk singer had made was a nasty ring from his brandy snifter on the MacLeish's 1785 cherry table. I'll never understand why Bob Dylan froze in front of Archibald MacLeish. Was it awe, or boredom? Whatever, it was a serious warning that I blithely ignored. It was a grim ride until we reached my home when Bob asked if he could stay for dinner. After eating, unexpectedly, he sang for his supper by performing all his golden oldies, and delight-ed us further by singing a duet ("Skeeball") with our eleven-year-old daughter, Julie. Looking back, I believe it was his way of tipping us. It was a joyous occasion and the last time I ever saw Bob Dylan.

Back to *Chronicles* and Dylan: "MacLeish tells me that he considers me a serious poet and that my work would be a touchstone for generations after me, that I was a postwar Iron Age poet but I had seemingly inherited something metaphysical from a bygone era. He appreciated my songs because they involved themselves with society, that we had many traits and associations in common and that I did-n't care for things the way he didn't care for them." Delusion.

In *Letters of Archibald MacLeish 1907 to 1982* (Houghton Mifflin, 1983) MacLeish wrote on 7 October 1970 to his editor: "Now as to Bob Dylan. He proved to be simply incapable of pro-ducing new songs, and things looked desperate until Ostrow decid-ed about a month ago to use old songs of Dylan's in spite of the fact that songs on Broadway are all supposed to be new. For one thing the

old songs are more to our purpose since Dylan has now entered advanced middle age, being almost thirty and no longer fiery: for another, they are far better than anything he is now doing."

I tried reaching Dylan for weeks, with no success. Was he ill? Did he have another motorcycle accident? MacLeish was in Antigua, attempting to complete his adaptation without Dylan's score, and Peter Hunt and I were deep into the set design. I had raised all the money, the theatre was booked, are we were poised to begin casting the moment Dylan showed up, when Clive Davis, then President of Columbia Records (and the man who introduced me to Bob Dylan), called: "Stu, Dylan's first album in three years, is on release tomorrow and it's a bitch; thanks, pal." Album? Bitch? Pal? What I had hoped for was a seamless collaboration: two American poets, dramatizing folklore with song. It was a risky idea from the start but when Bob Dylan betrayed us, 79-year-old Archibald MacLeish was devastated. Although I knew better, I produced *Scratch* as a play to repay MacLeish for his trust in me. *New Morning*, an album by Bob Dylan: Columbia Records #PC30290, was released December 17, 1970. *Scratch*, a play by Archibald MacLeish opened on Broadway, at the St. James Theatre, Thursday May 6, 1971, and closed May 8, 1971. *Requiescat in pace*, Archie. As for you Dylan, the answer is blowin' in the wind.

7

STEPHEN SCHWARTZ AND ROGER O. HIRSON

PIPPIN

Pippin was irreverent, funny, hip, and sexy; a take-off on a young man's search for fulfillment; a parody of war, parents, Crusades, old age, monogamy, religion, and suicide. It was the right show for the seventies, ran for five years and in 1977 became the tenth-longest running musical of all time. Here's how it happened. My hopes to produce a contemporary musical which would appeal to a new generation of theatregoers on Broadway were dashed in 1971 when I failed to deliver Bob Dylan's songs intended for *Scratch*. That's when Stephen Schwartz, recently graduated from Carnegie-Mellon University, came to my Broadway office to play his score to *Pippin*. Dressed in the hippie uniform of the day (stained glass print shirt tails over chinos) and sporting a shoulder length hairdo, Stephen was the embodiment of self-confidence bordering on arrogance. He reminded me of me when I was twenty, nose and all, and from the moment he played "Corner of the Sky" I knew Stephen was the new voice I was looking for. The rest of the score was just as fresh and when he told me it was Carole King who most influenced his music, I felt the earth move under my feet and agreed to produce it on the spot. Stephen had written *Pippin* as a CMU project (along with Godspell, which was about to open Off-Broadway) and his book was a college jape. His agent had enlisted Roger O. Hirson (*World War 2½*) to rewrite the text and the three of us spent the next year trying to make it work.

Enter Bob Fosse. I first played poker with Fosse when he was married to Mary-Ann Niles. He had the same gimmicks then and could bluff you with a pair of deuces. Dressed in black, from his socks to pork-pie hat, smoking a dangling Camel cigarette, he'd give you that baby-face deadpan stare so you weren't sure if he was going to slug you or kiss you if you dared call his hand. We subsequently worked together on *The Girls Against the Boys*, a revue he was called in to doctor and *How to Succeed in Business Without Really Trying*. When I left

Frank Loesser to produce *We Take the Town,* Fosse was my choice to direct my first solo musical and although he turned me down, he came to Philadelphia to offer encouragement. (I was to return the favor, and a lot more than encouragement, 14 years later for *Chicago.*) In 1971 he had just returned from Germany, having wrapped the film version of *Cabaret* and was directing the TV special *Liza with a Z,* when I offered him *Pippin.* He thought Stephen's musical was "a piece of ———" but since he hadn't directed on Broadway for years he would agree to take it on only if I paid him a $25,000 advance. It was the best investment of my career. It wasn't until Bob Fosse said he would direct that the tone of the musical changed from a sincere, naive, morality play to an anachronistic, cynical burlesque.

The turning point came when we created a character called The Leading Player (Fosse had Ben Vereen in mind), a con man from the 1970s in the 9th century, who would narrate and manipulate *Pippin* using showbiz magic. Anything to do with magic fascinated Stephen (he would later write a score for *The Magic Show*) and he responded immediately to the suggestion that he write an opening number for the character. Miraculously he wrote "Magic To Do" over the weekend. A bluesy, mysterious vamp introduced the song, inspiring Tony Walton to design a light curtain where all you could see were disembodied hands and Ben Vereen's face, followed by a hip rhythmic chorus with playful eighth-century lyric references. It foreshadowed the events of the evening (à la "Comedy Tonight"), cleverly balancing the Leading Player's Master of Ceremonies' showbiz savvy with Holy Roman Empire asides. An opening number in a musical is as essential as breathing out and breathing in and you must have one to survive. It proclaims the tone, topic, time, genre, language, and level of humor, energy, lunacy, and exhilaration you may expect for the rest of the evening. If it's a great opening number i.e.,

"Tradition," "Fugue for Tinhorns," "Rock Island," etc., the audience will trust you for the next twenty minutes while you plant the (albeit boring) necessary exposition that will eventually bring the story to light.

Throughout the next few months Bob came to our home in Pound Ridge, each visit with a gorgeous new babe, to "fix" (his word) the show. It was exciting walking the undulating hills (and ogling the undulating babes), talking dramatic structure, new songs, and production numbers, but even more so returning to join the playmate of the month for a swim in the pool. What we discovered worked best for *Pippin* were anachronisms. Anything that could lampoon the earnestness of the book (and deflate Schwartz's ego) would delight Fosse. In an interview with the *New York Times* Bob said of Schwartz: "He is talented but not as talented as he thinks he is." The animosity between them was manifest during the *Pippin* auditions when Fosse chose dancers rather than singers (notwithstanding songwriter Schwartz's strenuous objections) but the climax came when Bobby picked Ann Reinking, a nonsinger and untested actress, but whose purity of line and extension would have made Pavlova envious. Schwartz drew the line; he would have none of it! Fosse turned to me and said: "Either I get my dancers or I quit." I sent Stephen home and Fosse, Reinking, and *Pippin* lived happily ever after. (Or at least until 2000 when Stephen tried in vain to revive *Pippin* without Fosse's direction and dances.)

That confrontation was a beginning of the many changes of style Fosse introduced and the first test of authority for the author vis-à-vis his director. Another time was when Stephen objected to Fosse's rehearsal staging of Irene Ryan's (Granny from television's *The Beverly Hillbillys*) big number "No Time at All," but when I assured him it would stop the show (it did) he replied: "Is that all

you care about?" Not surprisingly I supported Fosse's concept of a dance show and the rupture between them never healed. (Nor has Schwartz ever accepted the Broadway version as his own and, not so incidentally, ever returned a penny of his bountiful royalties.) In fact when the printed version of *Pippin* was published, Stephen restored 67 of his college japes and eliminated most of the impertinent, hip, cynical, and proven laugh lines we had interpolated into the Broadway version For example, when Lewis, Pippin's overbearing brother, boasts to Charlemagne he slew twenty Frisians and is going to slay even more Visigoths, he asks rhetorically, "Right, Father?" This cues Charles to turn to the audience in disdain and pose the question: "Why do I always get nauseous when he calls me Father?"

Then there was the deletion of the entire antiwar section of "Glory," and the Leading Player's disc-jockey style announcements of catastrophic casualties from various wars, "still on the charts." What followed was the Manson Trio dance with Ben Vereen, Candy Brown, and Pam Sousa, which became the revolutionary television commercial (thanks to Blaine-Thompson's Ingram and Jeff Ash) and changed the way Broadway musicals would be advertised in the future. I could cite Schwartz's other 65 Carnegie-Mellon restorations, but you get the picture.

Rehearsals went very well and when we had our gypsy run-through at the Imperial Theatre Fosse invited his buddies Paddy Chayefsky and Herb Gardner. It was Chayefsky who contributed the Leading Player's finale entreaty to Pippin to self-immolate: "Why (it's) the final affirmation of life…death! " (Don't look for it in the published version.) Roger Stevens invested $100,000 in the production in exchange for my agreement *Pippin* would be the inaugural-commercial production at the recently completed Kennedy Center Opera House and I raised the balance of the capitalization from

Motown Records, which was accomplished with the crucial guarantee of a Michael Jackson recording of "Corner of the Sky." When the record was released Stephen was outraged because Jackson changed a lyric reference to children sitting in the snow to "Children *sit in the show.*" The song, however, became a smash hit, bolstering our advance box office sales. It was indicative of Stephen Schwartz' character to be steadfast in his authorship and although we opened in Washington D.C. to rave notices he thought his CMU baby was being perverted into a Broadway whore. (Much to his credit he continued to write the new songs I asked for: "On the Right Track" and "Love Song.")

The Kennedy Center opening was auspicious and we knew it from the first laugh John Rubinstein got when he appeared in a side theatre box before the curtain rise, asking the pit conductor where the stage was. (The bit was dropped in New York.) I've emphasized the beneficial effect of a great opening number, but after that, you'd better have another showstopper! Conceived in Sophie Tucker's half-talking style, "No Time at All, " did exactly that. It was due in part to Bob Fosse's, "follow-the-bouncing-ball effect," and Irene Ryan's outrageous mugging, but mostly because Stephen wrote an infectious tune and a humorous take on growing old. Furthermore, Schwartz cleverly kept Berthe, Charlemagne's aging mother (Ryan), in character despite her ribald jests.

Irene Ryan was a test of my relationship with Bob—he didn't want to cast her—but I was convinced Granny's vaudeville background was an asset and her television celebrity would help us at the box office. His unsentimental way of telling me I was right—after my refusing to let Stephen change his staging of her number—was when Fosse won his Tony Awards for *Pippin*, he sent me a dime-store trophy stenciled "Best Assistant Choreographer." Irene kept forget-

ting her lines during rehearsals, much to Bob's displeasure and my reassurances it would pass, nevertheless five months after our Broadway opening there were still moments on stage when she would dry. When Irene called me to her hotel one afternoon to ask me to replace her, I was furious thinking Fosse had finally gotten under her skin. I was mistaken. She told me she had secretly suffered a stroke during our rehearsals last September and didn't tell a soul for fear she would be taken out of the show. "I just want to be in a big hit Broadway musical before I die," she said. We had a good cry and she made me promise not to tell the company until after her final performance. Irene Ryan died the next month.

Carole King's influence on Stephen Schwartz was never more honestly realized than in his rhythmically complicated, yet oddly flowing, and soft rock, "Love Song," which was written to make the relationship between Pippin and Catherine plausible. It was a tricky duet to perform and added to Jill Clayburgh's dilemma as to whether or not to quit the musical. (Jill was an insecure singer and I'll always be grateful the song, and John Rubinstein, gave her the confidence to stay.) Bob Fosse never trusted the *Pippin* writing, which is why he staged the show as a circus, ballet, musical comedy, minstrel show, rock concert, magic, and vaudeville spectacle. With "Corner of the Sky," however, he knew the song evoked a yearning for fulfillment with the yuppie seventies' audience and had a million dollar refrain, so he didn't try to fix it. He merely put Pippin in a spotlight and let him soar.

Bob Fosse was at war with himself. He was into three packs of Camels a day, pills to help him sleep, pills to wake him up ("It's Showtime!"), booze, broads (sometime in tandem), and other stimulants not yet known to amateurs. Bob was self-destructing, burning himself out in order to resurrect a phoenix. During our

Washington D.C. tryout he came to me for solace. "Jesus, Stu, look at me. I'm falling apart. What should I do?" Although Fosse always told this story as a gag, I've never forgiven myself for my reply: "Just keep on doing what you're doing Bobby; we're going to be a hit!" Ugh.

Work was the ultimate narcotic and the more Fosse force-vomited before rehearsals the more the creativity flowed, so to speak. Leaving Washington for New York was just as bizarre. A death threat was made on Fosse's life by a jealous boyfriend of one of the *Pippin* chorus girls and I had to ask my connection at the White House to have the secret service escort us to the D.C. city limits. During previews at the Imperial Theatre I hired two off-duty NYPD to guard the rehearsals until a smart detective told me Fosse and the chorus girl were getting their kicks out of all the attention and the way to stop the nonsense was to fire the girl. I did and she returned the next day, with a black eye from her boyfriend, his honor apparently satisfied, and the threat was withdrawn.

There were a rash of youthful musicals in the 1972–73 season; *Grease*, celebrating the fifties, and *Dude*, from the creators of *Hair*, rejoicing The Highway Life, and then there was *Pippin*. The smart money on Broadway didn't give us a chance and a day before we opened at the Imperial Theatre the Shubert lawyers asked my permission to sell their $20,000 investment. So much for faithfulness.

Traditionally on opening night our family waited for the reviews in the George M. Cohan booth of the Plaza Hotel's Oak Room. My philosophy is, give me the luxuries of life and I will willingly do without the necessities. In other words, if we're a flop at least we'll go to the poorhouse well fed. (It was my friend Jerry Bock who admonished me the opening night of *The Apple Tree* to ignore the reviews and never forget the excitement of having created a new

1. *We Take the Town*, Peter Larkin (1962)

SET DESIGNS

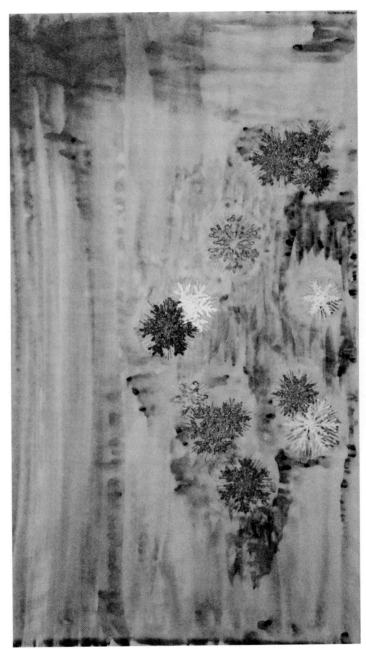

2. *Here's Love*, William and Jean Eckart (1963)

3. *The Apple Tree*, Tony Walton (1966)

PRESENT AT THE CREATION

4. *1776*, Jo Mielziner (1969)

5. *Scratch*, John Conklin (1971)

SET DESIGNS

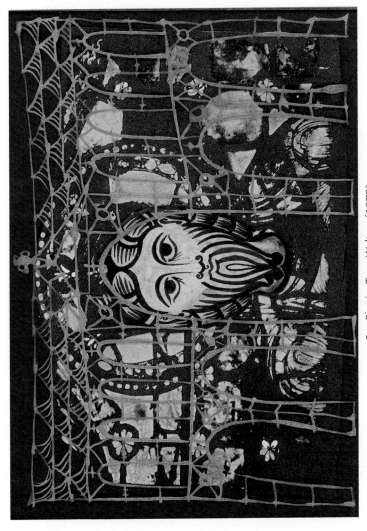

6. *Pippin*, Tony Walton (1972)

7. *M. Butterfly*, Eiko Ishioka (1988)

SET DESIGNS

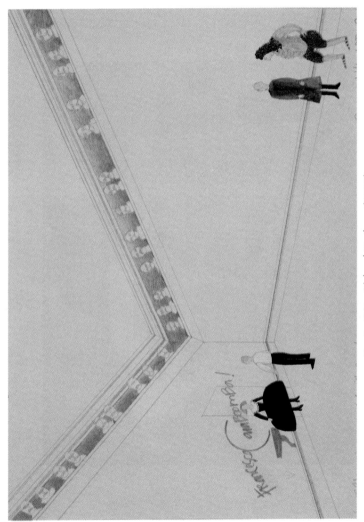

8. *La Bête*, Richard Hudson (1991)

work.) When Harvey Sabinson, our press agent, called The Plaza and told us the *New York Times* was a pan, we toasted farewell to the evening with a bottle of 1961 Château Lafitte and went to The Times Building on 43rd Street to pick up the first edition of the morning paper—in what now seemed *a very extravagant rented limo*. The Times review was a rave! Sabinson had convinced the first-string critic to change one word in his appraisal—from "flawed" to "sexy"—and the rest was a money notice. Thank you, Jerry and Harvey.

I awarded the London production of *Pippin* to Robert Stigwood, a knowing Brit who began his career with Brian Epstein (manager of The Beatles), because Bob Montgomery, a Paul Weiss attorney I admired, represented him. Stigwood proved to be an absentee co-producer, leaving the essential hands on responsibilities to his gormless General Manager who hated anyone from America. Which made it especially tough since I also had to direct the London Company until Fosse arrived for the final preview week. Bloody Scrooge had us rehearse in an ice-cold empty theatre in Brixton, considered to be the suburban dregs of London. After four weeks of freezing rehearsals, and two street muggings, we moved to Her Majesty's Theatre in the West End for our opening, and it was only then that Robert Stigwood appeared. He was apologetic and to make amends he opened the green room backstage and stocked it with the best booze, wine and hors-d'oeuvres The Savoy Hotel could transport to each preview performance. All that was missing were the call girls. For two glorious weeks Fosse and I were sybarites, tasting the high life before the show went on, at intermission and after the final curtain. The day after *Pippin* opened to sorry reviews we needed the green room more than ever, but found it *padlocked*. (*Pippin* didn't repay England for the loss of her colonies and the

Brits knew how to say bugger off.) All in all, *Pippin* made a lot of money, invented the Broadway TV commercial, won five Tony Awards and won over a chubby girl from Long Island in the 70s to be *Pippin*'s first groupie. Her name was Rosie O'Donnell.

8

JOHN KANDER AND FRED EBB

CABARET
CHICAGO

There were so many musicals in the fifties and sixties that an aspiring musical dramatist could learn to develop his craft in much the same way apprentice artists did in the Renaissance by grounding colors, priming wooden panels, making brushes of hog's hair, and learning such technical skills as casting and soldering. Kander and Ebb, Adler and Ross, Bock and Harnick, and Adams and Strouse all learned their craft by coaching singers, writing dance arrangements, pop songs, and revue material before collaborating on Broadway. This apprentice-master system all but disappeared in the seventies because fewer new, original musicals were being produced. The first time I heard Fred Ebb audition a score was for a musical he wrote with Paul Kline, in the late fifties, *Morning Sun,* and I recall a shy, rather nervous man who delivered an intensely emotional performance. I had the same experience listening to the audition of *Cabaret,* when I was a member of the Theatre Guild Subscription Committee. Fred Ebb was one of those songwriters who could wring the tears out, and play naughty with a lyric. He was so good that performers mimicked his style. Composer John Kander set Fred's *Cabaret* lyrics perfectly and together they established the team's métier: nightclub acts, roller rinks, burlesque, vaudeville, dance marathons—in essence, showbiz. *Cabaret* had the musical echo of Kurt Weill and the look of George Grosz' depraved Berlin; replete with prostitutes, fat Junkers, smug bourgeoisie, sottish drinkers, lechers, and hypocrites. "Willkommen," the musical's opening number, set the period and style of the show brilliantly and Boris Aronson's nightclub set of distorted (mylar) mirrors established the danger and decadence of prewar Nazi Germany. It was such a powerful moment the rest of the show never worked as well outside the cabaret atmosphere. The sinister M.C. of The Kit Kat Klub set the decadent tone of 1930s cabaret by dancing and romancing an on stage mock-gorilla with "If

You Could See Her." In the song's coda, reminding us of the period, farce turns to terror when he tells us she doesn't look Jewish. "Tomorrow Belongs to Me" was another sobering reflection of what the Nazis had in store for the world. Combination hymn ("Deutschland Uber Alles") and Goethe nature poem; an Aryan youth begins the insistent refrain, which is repeated by his country-men with such force that we are compelled to see, hear, and almost smell the evil. The show's title song "Cabaret" was an instant hit, momentarily liberating America from it's anti–Vietnam War demon-strations and Black Power threats, and celebrating Timothy Leary's dictum: turn on, tune in, drop out.

Cabaret was Harold Prince's best directorial job to date but it was overshadowed by Bob Fosse's movie version starring Liza Minnelli, both of whom owed their Broadway debuts to Prince. The only thing wrong with this wonderful production was it beat out The Apple Tree for the season's Best Musical Tony Award. The musical was revived in 1998, directed by Sam Mendes with co-direction/chore-ography by Rob Marshall, and eclipsed the 1966 version with new dances and decadence in a reconverted Henry Miller Theatre with cabaret seating, renamed "The Kit Kat Club." It wouldn't be the only time Rob Marshall would triumph by reinventing Bob Fosse. I first saw Marshall's choreography in the 1980s in Pittsburgh when he was "Wingtips" in The Park Players' production of Noodle Soup. Rob was a close friend and classmate of my daughter Julie Ostrow at Carnegie-Mellon University and he burned with ambition and talent. We became an extended family over the next two decades and shared heartbreaks and hits, but none more serendipitous than his joyous direction of the 2003 movie version of Chicago.

In 1975 when Bob Fosse was compelled to have a heart bypass and postponed directing, Chicago, Paddy Chayefsky, Herb

Gardner, and I were regular visitors at New York Hospital where the operation was to be performed. Fosse asked Chayefsky to read his will and when Paddy discovered he wasn't mentioned, he screamed: "You son-of-a-bitch, LIVE!" I also recall the day of the operation, Gwen Verdon calling and telling me Bob had left me $10,000 to throw a wild party in the event he died. I told Gwen to tell him I would do it for $5,000. (She did, and Bobby laughed all the way to the operating room.) Fosse was weak from the ordeal, yet returned to direct *Chicago* because he felt he owed it to Gwen. It was much too soon and I wasn't surprised when after a rocky opening in Philadelphia he asked if I would help him fix the show; my billing to be, "Associate Friend." Fosse gave me 1% of his royalty (rising to 1-1/2% on recoupment) and a major headache; I was trying to pull together all the insecure passions of the authors, stars, and producers, who felt they were being abandoned. Fortunately the original *Pippin* designers, musical and backstage staff, and former chorus members—all now involved in the creation of *Chicago*—stood in the path of their friendly fire and urged me to help them save the show. There was so much that was brilliant in the musical: a great score, a unique form, a dynamite cast and dance numbers to stop your heart; *Chicago* didn't need saving so much as it needed editing.

It must have been John Kander's experience as a dance arranger that inspired him to compose some of the best vamps in musical theatre history: "Willkommen" from *Cabaret*; *Zorba*'s "Life Is," and the seven quarter-notes followed by a dotted sixteenth-note pick-up made the vamp to "All That Jazz" from *Chicago* the best. (It was so good Marvin Hamlish wrote a variation on it for "One" from *A Chorus Line*.) Vamps are gateways to a song, insistent musical suspensions telling you something wonderful is coming. And Kander and Ebb didn't let us down with their brash 1920 Chicago-

Dixieland-Creole-Jazz-Band opening number. W. C. Fields's tombstone read: "Better here than in Philadelphia," and no wonder; trying out a musical in the city of brotherly love could be deadly business. "All That Jazz," was staged on a rising elevator from the orchestra pit (the band was on stage), and one night the elevator fell from the stage level down the trap to the basement. Fortunately no one was hurt, but the show was canceled that evening. I'll never forget the next day's performance and the shaken but gallant Chita Rivera; rising in view on the repaired elevator, singing Ebb's masterful period reference lyrics and holding on to the newly installed hand railing for dear life!

Staged as a cynical vaudeville show (M.C. and all), each character had their stage turn. "Mister Cellophane," was written for a cuckold husband, and as played by Barney Martin, Amos was the only character in the musical you really cared for. Fred Ebb and Fosse gave Martin the shambling stage persona of Bert Williams —top hat, shabby dress suit, very large shoes—and most significantly, with a wonderful Kander slow ragtime refrain, reinvented William's trademark song, "Nobody."

Chita Rivera said they called Bobby and me, "Gloom and Doom," because of the cuts and new musical numbers I asked to be put into the show. Kander and Ebb wrote "When You're Good To Momma," under duress, since it required eliminating their favorite character, an agent (played by David Rounds), and the song "Mr. Ten Percent." Rounds wrote to thank me after being fired and landing the starring role (now legendary) in the musical *Herringbone*. It was difficult enough for Fosse having to fire an actor (he was always insecure of being fired himself) but putting, "Nowadays," in as a new finale for Gwen and Chita, was a heart scald. We were in the musty downstairs Forrest Theatre bathroom lounge, the only other place to rehearse while the stage was being used, and Fred and John had just

finished playing their new song. It was a sardonic duet, replacing a not-so-funny (nor musical) drum and saxophone bit by the two stars. Both ladies were delighted, but when we asked Gwen to start the song, she announced "Nowadays," would be sung as a single, *by her.*

The smell of fear filling the room was even stronger than the disinfectant smell of the men's room urinals, and a cue for Kander and Ebb to disappear. "This is mine, Fosse," said Gwen, " No more for the good of the show. It's mine!" By now Chita was in tears, imploring me to give the number to Gwen, and Fosse was dazed. (He later told me he wanted to quit, then and there.) I quickly sat our dance arranger Peter Howard at the piano and asked him to play the song and ignore the hysterics. Peter began playing and Gwen, now also crying uncontrollably, yet not leaving, started the song! Chita, hearing her, came to the piano, and through her tears sang her part of the duet. During what seemed like an eternity, the tears stopped and the two stars sailed into the second chorus; now laughing and hugging each other. After it was over and all was forgiven and forgotten, except by me, I turned to Bobby and said: "I want 2%." The show was a modest hit (eclipsed by the Off-Broadway opening of *A Chorus Line*) and after a few months of receiving Fosse's promised royalties (our gentleman's agreement), he said I was rich enough and stopped paying me. "Everything about it is appealing...." And all that jazz.

If Bob Fosse ever needed a theme song it would have been, "Razzle Dazzle"; because the dialogue he and Fred Ebb wrote for the character of the showbiz-lawyer, Billy Flynn, came straight from his crooked heart. Bobby told me he thought of himself as "a fraud with a couple of good dance steps." He was a genius, of course, and died much too soon, leaving a creative musical theatre legacy second only to Jerome Robbins. I once wrote a line for Bob

Fosse in the movie, *All That Jazz*, which he loved: "I always look for the worst in people, and usually find it." His tragedy was wanting to believe it.

9

STUART OSTROW

STAGES

Pippin and *Chicago* were established stage hits when Bob Fosse suggested we continue our partnership in the movies. He told me I'd love Hollywood, producing films and making certain he threw up before each take. At the time I was writing my first play, *Stages*, encouraged by Stephen Sondheim who generously acted as my dramaturge. Elisabeth Kübler-Ross's *On Death and Dying* inspired the play and I still can remember the creative exhilaration of being more than "someone who knows a writer." I *was* the writer! Sam Cohn, Fosse's canny agent, and Barry Diller, then head of Paramount Pictures, kept nipping at my heels to come up with an idea for Bob's next movie. I found a four-character book by Hilma Wolitzer, entitled *Ending*, also about death and dying, which I thought would stretch Fosse to direct a string quartet, rather than a symphony orchestra of a film, and also would help me write my play. Both assumptions were wishful thinking. I hired Robert Alan Arthur for $30,000 to write the screenplay and sold it to Diller for a budget of three million dollars.

When we arrived on the Gower Paramount lot, Bob and I were given the Sam Spiegel-Elia Kazan bungalow, used by them during the filming of *The Last Tycoon*. Bob Fosse was the reason for Diller's green light, so naturally he took the larger (Spiegel) office, but I was thrilled at the thought of working in Kazan's space; he was a theatre giant I greatly admired. Screen stars paraded in daily, for cocktails and "chats," until I asked Bob when we were going to have them audition. Bob replied they had been auditioning; we didn't have to hear them read the part because" it was all in the eyes." It suddenly dawned on me I was in a la-la-land that had nothing to do with my theatre experience. It was all about being photogenic, and shooting enough film so the director could create any performance he wanted, simply by editing. What was I doing here? The coup de théâtre happened the next day. As I drove into my parking space, *the*

Paramount custodians were stenciling my name, in yellow paint, over Gage Kazan's! I couldn't breathe and called Sam Cohn to tell him I was leaving for New York that afternoon and that Bob could have my share of the picture. Immersing myself to complete *Stages* and self-producing it on Broadway (a grave miscalculation) with Richard Foreman directing, momentarily restored my equilibrium. Audiences for the thirteen sold-out previews were thrilled and I recall our casting director, Scott Rudin, telling me it was the best new play he had seen in years. On opening night however the Broadway establishment hated it and I knew we had closed during the first act. Years later, Edward Albee said I should have used a fictitious name: "They would never let a producer think he could write." The kicker was that *Ending*, the intimate movie I commissioned about a young married man dying in a hospital became *All That Jazz*, a musical extravaganza about Fosse's heart attack. Bob's film career stayed alive by his dying on screen, my writing career died by trying to stay alive on stage.

In February 1978 the *New York Times*, as was their tradition in advance of a Broadway opening, asked Richard Foreman and I to write individual think pieces about *Stages*. Ominously, neither article appeared in the Sunday Arts & Leisure section the weekend before our March 19th opening. Obviously the *Times* knew something we didn't know. So for the record here they are, Ostrow first:

My compulsion to write began in 1974 at the time the Musical Theatre Lab was established. Suddenly I was involved with experimental musical workshops, producing four and five each season at St. Clements Church and later on at the Kennedy Center. The dream had become a reality, it worked, and there was an exciting place where new musicals could be nurtured without the immediate pressure of box office and reviews. Anything was possible. As a producer I've learned theatre tends

to confirm new ideas that are already in the air rather than originate them, and what was in the air then was the fascination with death and dying as a theme. As Anatole Broyard observed, we seemed to have grown weary of the story and wanted to cut to the end. I was convinced a musical that could sing and dance about dying—treating the subject in metaphor, attempting to bring us closer to the truth by disguising the reality of what mystifies us most—was theatrical and timely. Perhaps it was because I couldn't interest any writer in taking on the assignment, perhaps it was because I had always wanted to write, perhaps it was the Lab environment, and, most likely, it was because I was forty-two years old that I decided to write the musical book myself. When I finished writing *Stages* three years, two bank loans and seventy-one bewildered ("Oh, you're writing a musical about *dying*...") stares later, it was a play. Song and dance had become farce and surrealism, slapstick and romantic melodrama.

Elisabeth Kubler-Ross's remarkable study *On Death and Dying*, which identifies five principal emotional "stages" terminal patients endure, motivated the form for the piece and Ernest Becker's eloquent discourse *The Denial of Death* where he states: "Whatever man does on this planet has to be done in the lived truth of the terror of creation, of the grotesque, of the rumble of panic underneath everything. Otherwise it is false," inspired its philosophy. Indeed, *Stages* is an attempt to dramatize helplessness in the face of panic.

The play is divided into five stages—acts, if you will—with one intermission. These stages are entitled Denial, Anger, Bargaining, Depression, and Acceptance. Each is a cumulative episode where the play's central character, The Actor, who is dying, experiences his condition. On one level the stages are five different situations The Actor must live through, on another, they are metaphors for his state of mind. For example, in the first stage, Denial, like the person who when he is first told he is

dying says, "No, not me—it cannot be true," the Actor, playing the role of a playwright, is faced with disastrous reviews on his opening night. When the first stage of denial cannot be maintained any longer it is replaced by feelings of anger and resentment. The logical next question becomes "Why me?" and in Stage Two, Anger, The Actor finds himself playing the role of a House Un-American Activities Committee witness, fighting for his life beyond the bounds of possibility or reason. In Bargaining, "O.K. I know it's me, but if I could just have a little more time…," his condition physically manifests itself and he bargains desperately for happiness. When the Actor can no longer deny his illness, when he begins to have more symptoms, becomes weaker, and cannot smile it off anymore, he enters the fourth stage, Depression. Now the metaphor reverberates with the American madness of vacation kingdoms and terminal hospital wards. In the final stage, The Actor is almost void of feelings. It is as if the pain had gone, the struggle is over. This is Acceptance, the moment of frail nobility only the helpless may attain, by hanging on. The odyssey to this Sunday has been joyful and painful, the joy due mostly to Richard Foreman's genius, Actor Jack Warden's artistry, and a corporal's guard of friends who put up with me and for me. I can't yet express how it feels about being both the playwright and producer of *Stages* except to say that both of us are very nervous.

Stuart Ostrow

Herewith, Richard Foreman's article:

I really had no idea who Stuart Ostrow was when, two years ago, just after I'd finished directing *Threepenny Opera* for Joe Papp, Stanley Silverman came to me carrying a script he'd been given by this man who's name vaguely rang a bell in the back of my mind—I knew he produced musicals—maybe with a partner, maybe not, and I had no ideas WHICH shows were his. So I asked. and was told, "Oh *Pippin, 1776 …*"

and having seen neither (I see on the average one Broadway show a year), I started browsing through the script of *Stages.*

Now I HAVE read a fair number of Broadway scripts friends had been carrying around when they were in rehearsal and I HAD been on various panels reading scripts submitted for grants and fellowships, and one thing had become self-evident. For a play to be commercially producible in New York at this point, it had to be a well-tooled product PURGED of all idiosyncratic, personal, private intensities and visions. It had to be a script that functioned exclusively within the public domain of a subject matter and dramatic style which would allow the Broadway public to say, "Oh yes , I've seen that before and this is a good version of it!"

For the last ten years, I and my peers have been functioning on the fringes of the commercial theatre, creating an alternative theatre off-Broadway in which the vision of the artist—in its most specifically individualistic moments—is the be-all and end-all of the work. Theatre neither of the marketplace nor of public forum, but theatre of communion in which one individual is telling what it feels like where he—one out of four billion—stands; and hoping that such truthful emotional information is in some way useful to whoever is out there in the audience.

Stuart Ostrow, powerful and successful Broadway producer, has functioned in a theatrical environment quite different; and indeed the "art" theatre, the experimental nonprofit theatre which now exists in America (and which for the rest of the world IS the current American theatre), came into existence and shaped itself often in specific opposition to that theatre which shaped and gave great success to Stuart Ostrow.

And yet, something bizarre happened. Apparently something was seething inside Stuart, and he started writing, and a play came out, and it was NOT the kind of play that can feasibly be produced on Broadway.

It WAS a play of intense, personal vision—a play of metaphor rather than plot, theme and variations rather than beginning, middle, and end—a play recreating the poetry of the theatre rather than reporting on and documenting something that ostensibly happens "out there" in the world.

Now, I read Stuart's play two years ago, and about two months later we met and he said, "Would you like to direct my play?" and I said yes, but what I didn't say was, though I was thinking it, "'Are you crazy?" Do you really think that a play like this, a play of poetry and craziness, which we all know about but refuse to recognize and acquiesce to unless it's "downtown" or in a loft somewhere or otherwise suitably framed as an experimental venture which is of course not in the mainstream (ha-ha) but acceptable as an example of how open we are to experiments and new things so long as they don't pretend to be CENTRAL...! Do you really think you can get away with doing a play like this in the commercial American theatre?

I didn't say it like that. I said, "Hummm, Stuart Do you, er, um...care-care if the audience leaves the theatre saying they weren't one hundred percent sure what it was they just saw?" And Stuart said he didn't care...so long as the energy and truth and vitality of his vision was there, offered to whoever would choose to be so open.

I don't think I really believed him at that time. I said to myself, "well, I have nothing to lose." I'm fascinated by the play because it's full of the concrete schtick of the theatre and schtick really means poetry, metaphor, primary-process energy! And the play organizes itself like poetry or music-talking about things (death, in this case), which can be most accurately spoken of through analogy because description gets in the way of true experiencing—and this play is the experiencing not the description. I need that kind of text to work on. So I'll do the play. Even though when it gets down to the crunch...maybe he'll find ME too pri-

vate in the associations and colors and inventions I can bring as a director and my intensities will interfere with his intensities. But it doesn't seem to be working out that way. I'm sure some part of the audience will say, "What was THAT about?" But they're getting the real thing—which doesn't often happen on Broadway. If they, you, critics, etc. like it or dislike it—that's one level of success or failure. But on a more significant level, Stuart Ostrow has pulled something off that involves courage, mostly, even more than talent (whatever that is: it's defined differently at different times and places).

Stuart told the truth... and then he did it on Broadway, where he risks everything. It's an "experimental" play and it's got a huge set and a big cast, etc,.., etc.—and he didn't have to take that risk. Except a few people, lucky ones, reach the point where the BIG risk beckons...and all other, safer options seem pale. And if the possibility of "art' exists on Broadway...well, to paraphrase, "It's by their risks...that you shall know them."

Richard Foreman

10

DAVID HENRY HWANG

M. BUTTERFLY

In 1986, Hal Prince and I were working on a crossover musical based on André Malraux's *La Condition Humaine (Man's Fate)* with composer Philip Glass and playwright, David Henry Hwang, when Prince received Andrew Lloyd Webber's offer to direct *The Phantom of the Opera*. Alarmed Prince would shelve our musical before I could get everyone under contract, I rushed to Paris, hired an avocat, and stormed the publisher Gallimard's office in hopes of obtaining the rights to the deceased author's novel. With an introduction from Prince, I managed to meet with Malraux's daughter, Florence (film-maker Alain Resnais' wife and co-executrix of her father's estate), who told me she was in favor of our adapting the novel but the power to decide was Gallimard's. (What she didn't say was her husband didn't care for Glass' music.) After several meetings in Paris it was clear Gallimard was not about to license their French demigod's master-piece to a Chinese-American and three New York Jews. In addition to their anti-Semitic and anti-American bias, French intellectuals think Broadway musical theatre is akin to the Folies-Bergere.

Everything happens for the best. Prince went on to direct *Phantom* and Hwang sent me a two-page proposal for a musical about a *New York Times* story of a French diplomat who'd fallen in love with a Chinese actress who subsequently turned out to be not only a spy, but also a man. In his afterword of the published play, David said "I remember going so far as to speculate that it could be some 'great, *Madame Butterfly*–like tragedy'. Stuart was very intrigued, and encour-aged me with some early funding." When David finished *M. Butterfly*, it was a play with Puccini's music, not the musical I thought I had commissioned. But after reading his drama concerning a former French diplomat and a Chinese opera singer who were sentenced to six years in jail for spying for China after a two-day trial that traced a story of clandestine love and mistaken sexual identity—the diplo-

mat, Mr. Gallimard, was accused of passing information to China after he fell in love with Mr. Song, whom he believed for twenty years to be a woman—I knew immediately I had to produce it on Broadway, and with John Dexter as the director.

John Dexter was forever sending me books. He was the best-informed man on the arts (all of them) I ever knew and his direction of *M. Butterfly* required I be as well prepared as he. The enemy was pretentiousness. Dawdling actors were told to "Get on with it," designers were ordered to make the costume or set change work better ("To hell with your Tony Award"), and when he met with a disgruntled lawyer representing my co-producer, who said," Change the script or I'll eat you up," John replied, "I'm indigestible." Indeed.

We had our troubles out of town and, as usual, everybody said, fix the lighting and fire the supporting actress. (In this instance it was the admirable Rose Gregorio.) "Certainly we made a casting mistake but the play works and we have a moral commitment to the lady," said Dexter. David Henry Hwang rewrote the part for Gregorio, the cast's morale soared, business in Washington improved and in the end everything came up roses, for she and for we. John Dexter was the real thing. He gave you answers you didn't always expect to hear and taught you to trust your conscience. John could also be petulant, or even cruel. One tense moment with the great director was when he insisted on the final day of auditions at the St. James Theatre that Brian Dennehy play the lead in David Henry Hwang's meditation on men and women, East and West, and appearance and reality. I thought Kevin Spacey had given the uncommon reading, but was too young, that Brian Dennehy was too much of an Irish mug to play a French diplomat, moreover that John Lithgow—who had called from his film location in Montana after reading *M.Butterfly*, beseeching me to be auditioned—had the androgynous

look of a sufferer and should be cast as Gallimard. Dexter and I walked around the block arguing (he threatened to quit) while the three actors waited for a decision. That's when Dexter let it slip he had dinner with Dennehy the evening before. My hunch was he had assured Dennehy the part was his (before seeing Lithgow's audition) so I told Dexter to go back to the hotel. I informed the actors the majority vote was for Lithgow and that Dexter had quit in protest. It was all a charade. PS: John Lithgow was nominated for the Best Actor Tony Award that year.

Dexter's cruelest moment was on the afternoon of our opening night, when after a brush up rehearsal he called B. D. Wong to the apron of the stage and said something like, "I want you to know that since rehearsals and all through our Washington engagement and previews in New York, your performance has been a disgrace. You mince around the stage like the faggot that you are and have yet to follow my direction; tonight is your last chance, "and then Dexter walked out of the theatre. John Lithgow and myself, the remaining witnesses who could bear listening to this attack, sought to comfort Brad but he would have none of it and stoically went to his dressing room. I was going to *kill* Dexter and contemplated canceling our opening, but it was 5:00 PM and our curtain was at 7:00. So I went to Wally's & Joseph's, belted down two stiff scotches and prayed for a miracle. (St. Malachy's Actors Chapel was next door to the bar.) Guess what? Brad gave the performance of his life and when I tried to reprimand Dexter for putting everything at risk, he simply said, "It's none of your business, I know my job." Indeed. I brought his Drama Desk and Tony Awards to London and staged a luncheon at the Savoy Grill amidst the splendor and festivity of nouvelle cuisine. "I'll have the Bangers and Mash," he said to the posturing maître d'. "Sorry, Stuart old

DAVID HENRY HWANG

91

boy, but you must know by now that I'm just a meat and potatoes man." Indeed.

I often wonder, if there was a musical around at the time which excited me as much, would have I have taken on this straight play? Suffice it to say, I imagined *M.Butterfly* as a musical on an epic scale, off the ground, and produced it accordingly. I hired an unknown Eiko Ishioka to design the production and when I suggested the *M. Butterfly* sweeping full stage ramp continue downward through the floor into a vomitorium, Dexter concurred and altered his planned exits and entrances to give the staging of the play a classical theatricality. I could never discover rigid method or policy in producing activities. It seemed to me that continually shooting arrows into the air, hoping that they might fall somewhere that counted, was a good thing. The idea is to be all over the place, poking your nose in everywhere, nipping at the heels of the creators, always prodding, like a very small shepherd dog, pushing them relentlessly, to some pasture, which you had decided would be good for them.

Not that all the artists I've encountered have been sheep. During the *M.Butterfly* tryout at the National Theatre in Washington, I said to David Henry Hwang: "I wish you would write a speech about deception." Coming out of a clear blue sky, the suggestion shocked David. He said, "What do you mean, Stuart?" "Oh, I don't know," I said. "Just a speech about delusion…deception." I've forgotten what David said, but I was certain he thought it was one of the silliest and vaguest ideas he had ever heard. Now the strange fact is that, two days later, he wrote a speech for the duped French diplomat who thought his lover was a Chinese opera diva. "I'm a man who loved a woman created by a man," the diplomat said, "to feel the curve of her face, the softness of her cheek, her hair against the back

of my hand," and then confessed, "I knew all the time somewhere that my happiness was temporary, my love a deception; but my mind kept the knowledge at bay, to make the wait bearable." There it was; a speech about deception! An arrow shot in the air. This, I submit, is producing. There is no way of learning how to do this in a college course. I don't know how to tell a young man or woman what to do in order to acquire the enthusiasm and haphazard hope necessary to transpose the slings and arrows of outrageous fortune into success. As for the business end of producing, it is necessary to be a kind of small Hercules, where no Augean stable is too big to clean if one has to clean it to get a show on.

Producing theatre today is very expensive. Partnerships, even with the devil, are necessary, and I had made a bargain with the Angel of Death. My first face-to-face meeting with David Geffen was for lunch, at Barbetta, on West 46th Street. It was some six months after the *M. Butterfly* Broadway opening and a few weeks since we had won the Tony Award for Best Play of the 1987–88 Season. It had been a tough, long journey—braving the storm in David Henry Hwang's skiff made of paper—and a triumph for those who refused to keep their dreams within reason. Not so, however for Geffen. He was my General Partner, but had not yet seen one performance of the celebrated production. Now, ten months later, we were enemies in arbitration suing each other for substantial violations of our Joint Venture Agreement, and the fancy fish Geffen had ordered for lunch wasn't going down with the white wine.

When I first asked him to read the play, to my delight, he responded by putting up a million dollars of the $1.5 million budget. What mattered to me more than the investment was the promise Geffen and I would work together. Michael Bennett had told me Geffen was helpful promoting *Dreamgirls* and I assumed his reputa-

tion as a hip record/music man would enhance the marketing of my risky play. *Not.* I knew something was seriously wrong with my decision when Geffen didn't show up in Washington for the National Theatre tryout, but sent his CEO instead (a Rolex-watched lawyer, with no professional theatre experience). I was momentarily relieved when after seeing two preview performances, the Rolex praised our work and flew off into the Western sunset. Then came the devastating Washington reviews; but not as threatening as the return of the Rolex, accompanied by his New York, Paul Weiss attorney. They demanded that we take out all the political references, all that "Brechtian bullshit" about Mao, and the Revolution. "Frank Rich will think it is pretentious," the connected lawyer-cum-oracle prosecuted, "It is, de facto, a love story between two men and that's box office! " Rolex added, "And if you refuse, Geffen won't give you a cent to bring it into New York."

Clearly, they had abandoned their belief in the metaphor of East and West that David had written and threatened Sunset Boulevard blackmail if we didn't accede to their prurient interests. I told David Hwang and John Dexter we were in bed with tyrants and the trick was not to get screwed. Box office business was terrible, but a genius director was focusing the writing and acting and the play was close to being realized. I went to the bank to mortgage our Pound Ridge home (without telling my wife) and loaned the Partnership $472,000, in order to get us to Broadway. Seven Tony nominations and Best Play Award, four Outer Critics Circle Awards for Best Broadway Play, the John Gassner Award for Best American Play, The Drama Desk Award for Best New Play, and one injunction later, *M. Butterfly* was the toast of the town and David Geffen was furious. Tyrants may forgive you for being wrong but they'll never forgive you for being right.

He was fashionably late for our lunch and wore a white T-shirt and jeans. Our conversation was pointless and the check came to $136.76. Geffen didn't carry a wallet (those tight jeans no doubt) so I used my credit card and gave him $20 cash for the tip.

He smiled: "Don't worry, you'll get it back," (I did, by messenger that afternoon), and as the aisle of waiters parted for him, he added that he thought *M. Butterfly* would be just a paragraph in his biography. (Geffen settled the arbitration by giving me 10% of his General Partner profits.)

Frank Rich's review was not what his Paul Weiss lawyer had predicted. "A major playwright.... *M. Butterfly* presents us with a visionary work that bridges the history and culture of two worlds...A brilliant play of ideas...David Henry Hwang's imagination is one of the most striking to emerge in the American theatre in this decade...One must be grateful that a play of this ambition has made it to Broadway." Rich's only cavil (and he was alone in this criticism) was he thought John Lithgow was miscast. Providentially, I offered David Dukes the part of Gallimard to follow John Lithgow. Having seen his unforgettable performance opposite Richard Gere in *Bent* I sensed his affinity to out-of-the-ordinary, dangerous theatre but worried he might take umbrage at replacing another actor. Wrong. Not only did he eagerly accept but he wasn't concerned John Dexter, our illustrious director, was unavailable and that I would direct his first appearance in the play. It became obvious during rehearsals why Dukes was so secure. He had a clear vision of how the character was to be interpreted—quite differently than Lithgow's, yet equally candid—and never once paid attention to anything I said. Thank God. His debut brought Frank Rich back to the Eugene O'Neill Theatre (in the fall of '89, after we had won the Tony Award for Best Play that June) when he eagerly revised his original review,

praising Dukes for bringing passion to the play. There were many other wonderful actors who followed. John Rubinstein, the original *Pippin*, was mature and touching, followed by Tony Randall. I was taken aback to read this in Randall's obit:

> He made clear, whenever he was asked, that his favorite role in more than 50 years of acting was that of a middle-aged French diplomat in the Broadway stage production of "M. Butterfly," David Henry Hwang's 1988 Tony winner. In it, Mr. Randall's character falls in love with a gorgeous Chinese woman who turns out to be a male spy in disguise. "It was the closest I ever came to being the kind of actor I believe in," he said on more than one occasion.—The New York Times 5/18/04

When I directed Randall in *M. Butterfly* (the fourth replacement) and nearly fired him because he insisted on playing Felix Unger and wouldn't play his age, I finally cracked his guise when he reluctantly agreed to take off his hairpiece. He then became Rene Gallimard. "Oh, now I see what you want, Stuart," Tony preened, and put the toupee back on. "What are you doing Randall?" I growled. "Don't worry Ostrow, I'll streak it gray." Actors.

Then there was Anthony Hopkins. My first choice to play Gallimard in the London production was Michael Gambon but Dexter wanted Tony Hopkins. Their relationship went back to *Equus*—when Dexter and Hopkins stormed against each other in the American premiere of Peter Shaffer's play—and perversely typical of Dexter he thought the animosity between them would create theatrical electricity. Instead we had a short circuit. Our tryout city was Leicester, an urban blight on the map of England where the best hotel in town was a Holiday Inn. Happily my London colleague Michael Codron recommended a four-star inn, Hambleton Hall, which was an hour's drive from Leicester but well worth the

trip. David Hwang and I settled in for four weeks of upper class English countryside living until a call from Anthony Hopkins, at four in the morning, shattered the idyllian tranquility. First, some background. When we met in Brown's Hotel in London Anthony Hopkins was charming, funny, warm and eager for any suggestions I had concerning his portrayal as Gallimard. (*How polite, I thought.*) Little did I realize Tony didn't understand the character. Over tea, we spoke of cabbages and kings and he volunteered a personal glimpse into his soul. He was an alcoholic (on the wagon), over-weight, fond of women dressers and makeup girls (but never his co-stars) an accomplished pianist, a lazy actor who was suspicious of directors, and thought working in the theatre was the pits. He loved making films (especially Hollywood movies) and was trying to make amends for his uninsurable booze binges in the motion picture business a few years back, by demonstrating sobriety on the legitimate stage. Ergo, *M.Butterfly.*

I blithely ignored Tony's unsuitability to play the part of a fragile, awkward man who is easily duped into believing the woman he was in love with for twenty years was a man; until five months later, Hambleton Hall, 4:00 AM. "Stuart, This is Tony. I'm leaving the show. Dexter is abominable! When he's not pontificating during those damn warm-up exercise sessions (Hopkins threw his back out the first day of rehearsals), or abusing the neophyte actors in front of the entire cast during rehearsals—he wants me to play 'gauche—I can't play bloody gauche!!" *B. D. Wong all over again,* I said to myself and convinced Tony to wait until noon (when rehearsals were to begin) for my phone call, after I had spoken with Dexter. Although I had my doubts about Tony's portrayal (and my hunch was so did he) I knew if Hopkins quit, the cast would follow and the production would close, so I seriously considered strangling John Dexter in

the men's room of the theatre. The hour's ride to Leicester however, calmed me, and turned my thoughts of murder to stratagem.

I met with John at 11:30 and told him of Hopkins' phone call, but instead of remonstrating with Dexter, I suggested we fire Tony. "After all, he is *miscast*—we both know it John—and so must he," I explained. "That's why he's so insecure with your style of directing." This time John didn't tell me, "It's none of your business, I know my job," rather, he called Tony and implored him to come to rehearsals. *Wherever I go, ego.* We opened in London at the Shaftesbury Theatre on April 20, 1989 and five months later (one month before Anthony Hopkins' contract was up) I ran into Tony one afternoon in St. James Park. We were a hit, selling out (mostly due to his celebrity) but the London reviews were mixed (mostly due to his characterization) and he was tired of *M.Butterfly.* "I finally have a movie offer," Hopkins told me. "It's a weird part but I'd like to take it if you'll release me from my contract." "Certainly Tony," I said, "I know you're unhappy." He was momentarily stunned at my unequiv-ocal reply but then…"Tell me Stuart, when did you first realize I was miscast?" "The first time was that day in Leicester when you let Dexter talk you into staying in the show," I answered. "But the clinch-er came a few months after our West End opening, when the running time of our show had accelerated from 2:40 on first night, to around 2:20, and I went backstage and asked you why you were rushing through the play and you replied: "I'm standing on stage thinking, 'Did I have an egg for lunch or ham?' And before I know it, the play is over." I'll never forget Tony smiling that crooked little grin and walking into the sunlit park following a crowd of tourists. The next time that image reoccurred was on the big screen when I watched a smiling Hannibal Lecter stalking his prey and anticipating dining on his liver, with some fava beans and a nice Chianti.

11

DAVID HIRSON

LA BÊTE

"The best laid schemes o' mice and men
Gang aft a-gley;
An' lea'e us nought but grief and pain,
For promis'd joy.
—Robert Burns

La Bête came in the mail in heroic couplets. My first reaction was to yawn, but my daughter Kate Ostrow—an English major recently graduated from the University of Michigan and struggling to live in the East Village—could use a readers fee, so I asked her for a breakdown of the play. Kate's previous critiques of musicals and plays were trenchant/scathing and I expected the same fate would befall *La Bête*. Imagine the chutzpah of its author, David Hirson, believing a commercial producer would produce an unknown author's impression of a seventeenth century comedy of manners! When Kate called me over the weekend and told me *La Bête* was the funniest play she had ever read—indeed when she said she and her roommate's laughter shattered a crystal ashtray while reading it aloud (we have the pieces on our memorabilia table)—it caught my attention. I was astonished by *La Bête's* form and language, and of course, the perversity of deviating from the correct Broadway fare has always intrigued me. But there was something else, a sense of unique theatrical scale, a feeling of being in another world, off the ground, which, as I discovered with *M. Butterfly*, was akin to producing musicals. Furthermore, both David Hirson and David Henry Hwang shared a Christian name, were both first-time Broadway playwrights (surely a sign) and I was still a stage-struck child, convinced there was an audience for risky theater. Therefore I began to scheme to bring it to Broadway. That was 1990, the beginning of an insipid decade, which would produce few new theatrical revelations and whose first casualty was the artistically ambitious *La Bête*.

In the early stages of collaboration when David and I pondered his text I told him I thought the ending of the play lacked hope. Elomire and Valere were locked in mortal combat and notwithstanding Elomire's intellect and eloquence, the fool Valere always prevailed. The dramatic situation was not unlike Benjamin Franklin's debates with his nemesis, John Dickinson, in 1776. In order for Dickinson to be more than a vanquished opponent we endowed his character with wit and wisdom equal to Franklin's, so that when he leaves the Continental Congress rather than betray his conscience by signing the Declaration of Independence, we salute him. David agreed and, much to his credit, after years of living alone with *La Bête*, had the courage to dismantle the whole house and start again. Weeks went by with assurances from David he was on to a solution. One must be reminded Hirson had a double-duty job when re-writing. He not only had to dramatize the scene and dialogue but then afterwards convert it all into iambs. Astonishing. Finally it was done. When David read me Elomire's thrilling speech ending the play as he takes leave from his patron, troupe, and safe haven rather than compromise his autonomy, I was moved. It was hope. Herewith, the last two quatrains:

Elomire:

Against great odds one gamely perseveres,
For nature gives advantage to a fool:
His mindless laughter ringing in your ears,
His thoughtless cruelties seeming doubly cruel;

His power stems from emptiness and scorn—
Debasing the ideals of common men;
But those debased ideals can be reborn…
By starting on the journey once again.

My only regret concerning *La Bête* is that we never attained the resigned yet inspiring majesty of Elomire's farewell speech on stage. Richard Jones and I fought over its interpretation. An American producer, I wanted more emotion. British director Richard wanted it ice cold. *La Bête* was the loser. Just as I knew when I read *M. Butterfly,* I wanted John Dexter to direct, Richard Jones was my first choice to direct *La Bête* and Richard Hudson to design it. I had seen their production of *Too Clever by Half* in London and was gob-smacked by its audacity and irreverence—the very qualities our nonconformist, critic bashing, intellectual, and thoroughly reckless play demanded. When Richard Hudson's "obtusely angled blazing white set" triggered the *La Bête* busts of Greek and Roman orators in the cornice of Elomire's (read Molière's) actors' cottage to rotate on cue, the lightning speed rhymes and iambs laughs that followed set the tone of the evening.

Both these British artists understood the elegance, wit and sophistication of the generic English comedy traditions, from Restoration comedy, Shakespeare, Sheridan, and Wilde, but neither, I was later to learn, possessed a sense of American stage energy and lunacy: its burlesque, gags, punch lines, and hellzapoppin' foolishness. This was never more apparent than in "The Parable of the Two Boys from Cadiz," a zany allegory performed by Valere for Prince Conti, the patron of Elomire's troupe. Instead of being hysterically funny it was merely bewildering, a schizophrenic reading of *The Three Stooges* by *The Crazy Gang.* Here's why. David Hirson learned his craft early on by watching the likes of *Pippin,* the musical I produced with a book by Roger O. Hirson, his father. He went from a Broadway brat to Yale, to a D. Phil., at Oxford—evolving into that rare amalgam of intellectual superiority and lowbrow shtick. David is an anomaly on Broadway and he has yet to find an American director who shares his background and talent.

When Andrew Lloyd Webber and Cameron Mackintosh won the Best Musical Tony for *The Phantom of The Opera*, David Henry Hwang and I won the Best Play Tony for *M. Butterfly*, and at the party afterwards Andrew graciously asked what I was producing next. I replied: "A comedy in rhymed couplets with a chandelier." He laughed and told me to call him when it was ready. I did, we lunched, and I gave him *La Bête* to read.

Two months later we met in Los Angeles at the Bel-Air Hotel, this time with his lawyer huddling close while we negotiated our partnership to produce David's "brilliant" (Andrew's adjective) play. "I'm told you have as large an ego as mine," Andrew grinned, "That means we'll get along smashingly." I smiled and replied, "Then you'll want your name, not your company's (The Really Useful Group) on our billing—'Stuart Ostrow and Andrew Lloyd Webber present'." His lawyer was troubled and cautioned Andrew against it. "Why so?" Andrew asked me, ignoring his counsel. "Ego, dear partner," I explained. "If the Broadway critics send us to the gallows we should hang together." Andrew agreed and was an exemplary partner—up until the end when I found myself alone in the tumbrel—the really useful lawyer having exacted his revenge. The exemplary part included Andrew hosting a reading of *La Bête* at his country estate in Sydmonton, England. Covering a vast expanse of beautiful landscape, Sydmonton was as Moss Hart once said of another high-living manor: "What God would have built if he had the money." Richard wasn't available so David Hirson and I rehearsed an impressive cast (including Alex Jennings as Valere) in London the day before our weekend in the country. Sydmonton was the British version of MGM's *Summer Stock:* with a bus ride from the West End to Andrew's 16th century church converted into a theater for upper class guests and a pool house for the actors to eat in and generally stay out of sight.

Mickey and Judy would have loved it but it demeaned the cast and instead of attending Andrew's elaborate luncheon before the show, I dined with the help. The morning's rehearsal lasted more than three hours and Andrew was worried his guests wouldn't last for that many rhyming couplets. When he requested I cut *La Bête* down I asked him which 12 bars could he eliminate from "Memory." We performed the entire play (with David and I seated in the last pew) and it was a disaster. Everyone thought it was going to be a musical—Webber previously initiated *Evita, Cats,* and *Phantom* at Sydmonton—and due to my hubris the audience went to sleep after the first act. Much to Andrew's credit he never reproached me, rather he said he loved the reading and sooner than have David and I endure another bus trip, he would send us back to London in his chauffeured limo. Class will tell.

I adore intelligent women. Meg Simon, of Simon & Kumin Casting was the kind of person you'd follow out of a burning building. Smart, tough, professional, opinionated, and feminine—"The next Ms. Ostrow," I announced. Meg assembled a cast for the Broadway production that is legendary: Michael Cumpsty, Tom McGowan, Dylan Baker, John Michael Higgins and Johann Carlo, just for starters. Jennifer Tipton, our lighting designer was a genius that could imagine the light at the end of the tunnel and take you through it—"The next Ms. Ostrow," I said—out of Meg's earshot. Both ladies played vital roles in the development of *La Bête.* Meg Simon's first choice for Valere was Robin Williams but he had a bad experience with the Mike Nichols/Lincoln Center production of *Waiting for Godot* and turned us down. Kevin Kline was interested but would only give us four months and finding an American actor with the chops for the starring role became a dispiriting task. After months of unproductive auditions an impatient Richard Jones

returned to London to stage a scratch and smell version of Prokofiev's opera *Love for Three Oranges*. It was at my instigation Meg, David and I went to London to ask Richard to audition Ron Silver for the lead. Although Meg and David had qualms about Silver I believed that the con-man quality he had conveyed in David Mamet's *Speed-the-Plow* (for which he won a Tony) would complement Valere's potential for mischief and harm. Wrong. The audition was scheduled for noon but when we all showed up at the Apollo Theater Richard asked to be left alone for an hour with Silver, presumably to direct him, which we all thought was strange since a star actor normally prefers to give a cold reading. In reality Silver had asked for help, a warning sign of his insecurity that I misinterpreted as nervousness. Instead, I took Meg and David to tranquil Cadogan Square for some sunshine and sustenance and had fish and chips with two wines, plonk and white.

When we returned to the theater Richard wanted another 30 minutes, so we waited, anticipating a great performance. Ron Silver's audition was tentative and unexciting and my heart sank—as did my stomach. I excused myself to the loo where I gave up my lunch. When we adjourned to my hotel to assess our situation (without Silver, whom we promised to phone) the amount of wishful thinking and rationalization that ensued was shameful. The truth is *all of us* were unsure, as well as being worried we'd never be able to cast Valere, so when I asked Richard if he could get a performance out of Silver he was equivocal, leaving the final decision up to me. I decided to hire him. When I called Ron to tell him the good news, he and his family were eating at a Chinese restaurant and invited us to join them for a celebration. We did, but afterwards and not unexpectedly, left starved.

The *La Bête* rehearsals at 890 Broadway went well except for Ron's growth as Valere. David, Richard and the cast were supportive of Ron but nervous when after four weeks he still didn't know his

lines. While Silver came to me the last week of rehearsals after a disastrous run-through and asked if I would like to replace him I attributed it to the usual actor jitters before a first public performance and encouraged him to open in Boston as scheduled. After ten days of technical rehearsals in the Wilbur Theater his agent called to say Silver wasn't ready and asked me to postpone the opening. By now Richard was a wreck and offered to leave. It was then I came to the realization this Silver would never perform regardless of how many hi-ho's I entreated. He missed all the previews and on opening night his understudy, Tom McGowan, went on and received rave notices. That caught Silver's attention and he finally performed the following evening. He was so unsure of his lines he arranged a code with an off-stage prompter to cue him when he recited the following couplet: "I do not want to disappoint the house, so let me get my next line from John Kraus." Upon hearing Ron utter this horrific ad-lib on stage Richard and David ran out of the theater and into the bar across the street. Needless to say I had to replace Ron Silver and haven't eaten any Chinese food since.

I called England to inform Andrew and the rapprochement between us was replaced by the whip of his lash: "You told me Ron Silver was going to be great as Valere," he charged, but calmed down when I reminded him he too had miscast and replaced Roger Moore, the lead in his musical, *Aspects of Love*. The confrontation with Ron Silver was to take place in his hotel suite and I asked Richard and David to join me. Jones was fainthearted and wouldn't attend—a mistake, which he paid for in the ensuing press imbroglio. David however was truly ill and begged off. I recall knocking on his hotel room door and insisting he bear witness. "It's a rite of passage to mark the arrival of your responsibility as an author," I said. "Silver will twist and turn, thinking I'm the only one who believes he is mis-

cast." David joined me and we left no turns unstoned. Silver and I agreed announcement would attribute his leaving as voluntary, due to "artistic differences," and that neither of us would talk to the press. I kept my word.

When Alex Witchel, the gossip reporter for *the New York Times* On Stage And Off column and wife of the Times drama critic, Frank Rich, printed the rumor that Ron Silver couldn't remember his lines (she got the news from another cast member, I later learned) and called me for confirmation, I wouldn't take her call. Silver (who was friendly with Witchell) however, had a field day; publicly accusing Jones of directing him to play the character gay, and suggesting I influenced a favorable *Boston Globe* review for the play and McGowan—as if anyone could manipulate the late, veteran critic, "Killer" Kevin Kelly.

Notwithstanding our excellent reviews the box office was as cold as the continuous snowstorms in Boston and we were running out of money. (Exacerbated in no small measure by Ron Silver's punishment that his contractual salary be paid for the for the run of the play.) Andrew came to Boston and was enchanted by the first act of *La Bête*, as well as with Tom McGowan's performance as Valere. We concurred that Tom should open the play on Broadway—and once more Andrew's largesse was manifest—he would advance $300,000 (which included loaning me my share of the additional capitalization) to bring us into New York. At the same time I received a $2,500 check from Jennifer Tipton, simply but grandiloquently declaring: "Let *La Bête* shine. Love, Jennifer." It was the first time in all my years of producing on Broadway that any creative collaborator put their money where their art was.

We opened at the Eugene O'Neill Theater February 10, 1991, two days late of my birthday and more than a dollar short.

The reviews varied from blissful to baffled to balderdash, bringing forth a legion of veteran theatergoers who long since had abandoned Broadway but who found hope for the original American play in *La Bête*. My investors were supportive—I raised an additional $125,000.00—and my friends rallied: Steve Sondheim encouraged: "You're a classy producer," Jerry Robbins came to see it twice and offered $25,000 to keep it running, Hal Prince urged the Lincoln Center Archives to film *La Bête* (they did) and more than two dozen luminaries signed a letter I instigated to the *New York Times* urging their audience to judge the play for themselves. My loyal investor's money had run out and Andrew's hit men told me to close the show. I painfully recall flying to Los Angeles to try to persuade the CEO and the *I-told-you-so*-lawyer for The Really Useful Group to lend me more money to keep the show running. I made an emotional speech about how I mortgaged our Pound Ridge estate to keep *M. Butterfly* running and quoting Teddy Roosevelt: "Far better it is to dare mighty things...than to live in the gray twilight that knows not victory nor defeat." To which the unforgiving lawyer added: "But most certainly will know bankruptcy."

We never overcame the damage from the controversial media attention and despite the many Tony nominations and awards for writing, design, direction, acting, etc., *La Bête* closed after 15 previews and 24 performances on Broadway. The search and destroy policy of the New York gossip media changed the rules of the game. In the past you went out-of-town to prepare the show for the New York critics and didn't advertise any favorable local reviews. In return, the Broadway press wouldn't write about the show until it was ready— after it came to New York—and you lived or died on what was written opening night. When the *Independent* in London called, asking for my comment on the occasion of *La Bête* winning the Olivier Award

for Best Comedy, I replied: "If I win any more awards for *La Bête*, I'll be totally bankrupted." Damn that lawyer.

12

ERNEST LEHMAN AND CLIFFORD ODETS

SWEET SMELL OF SUCCESS

Literature has been a great resource for musical theater. For *Guys and Dolls* the authors musicalized a short story by Damon Runyon, "The Idyll of Sarah Brown" into a full-length theater classic. Many other musicals were adapted from books; *Anna and the King of Siam* (*The King and I*), *Memoirs of Gypsy Rose Lee* (*Gypsy*), *Don Quixote de la Mancha* (*Man of La Mancha.*) Plays have also been the inspiration for musicals: Pygmalion (*My Fair Lady*), *Romeo and Juliet,* (*West Side Story*), *The Matchmaker* (*Hello Dolly!*) What hasn't worked as well is the concept of transforming a film to the stage. Garbo's, *Ninotchka,* was far more romantic than *Silk Stockings* and Leslie Caron's *Lili,* more heartbreaking (and hit-song making "Hi-Lili, Hi-Lo") than *Carnival! Promises, Promises* suffered a similar fate not only because the stage cast couldn't compete with the memory of Jack Lemmon and Shirley Maclaine in *The Apartment,* but also because screenplays are merely blueprints for the director, cinematographer, and film editor to shoot reels of reality, close-ups, and POV reactions in order to tell a story. Once these images are reflected on the screen the studio executives edit the dialogue and the outcome is just a representation of the narrative.

Theatre requires conflict, character, and catharsis and that begins and ends with words, not pictures. Coincidental with the waning of original musical works, the new millennium opted again for musical film adaptations—*The Full Monty* and *The Producers* being the most commercial—heralding the era of live motion pictures on Broadway. *Sweet Smell of Success* in 2002 was the new kid on the block. I was first attracted to the movie in 1957 when I was head of Frank Music Corp.'s Hollywood office, having worked my way up the ladder from a lowly song-plugger. (**Song-plugger** n. [originally U.S.] a person employed to popularize songs, especially by begging orchestra leaders, singers, and disc jockeys to perform them repeatedly.) Not unlike *SSOS*'s Sidney Falco (Tony Curtis) who was Ernie

Lehman and Clifford Odets' anti-hero press agent willing to sell his soul for a plug in J. J. Hunsecker's (read Walter Winchell's) gossip column; I was 28, wore slotted-collar white oxford shirts, tied a Windsor knot, smoked Chesterfield cigarettes, talked fast, hustled clients, two-timed girls, and shelled out payola to get my plugs. Sidney made me both want to cheer and hate myself for it, but his way of speaking was the stuff songwriters die for and if they're exceptional, will translate into soliloquy.

I had a little more than passing interest in *Sweet Smell of Success,* as the following evidence will testify. I decided to try making it a musical and approached the great jazz composer Johnny Mandel ("Emily") to write the score and Susan Birkenhead (*Jelly's Last Jam*) to write the book and lyrics, and Lindsay Anderson (*Oh Lucky Man!*) to direct. I knew Ernie Lehman from my days on the West Coast but when he brought in movie mogul David Brown, I withdrew. (The "BG" referred to in my September 1993 memo below is Barry Gray, a unique entertainment/political talk show host, who crossed Winchell in the fifties and was crucified by WW as being a "Commie." I wanted to dramatize Gray being Winchell's daughter's (not sister's) lover as the subplot.

27 SEPTEMBER 1993

TO: ERNEST LEHMAN   CC: DAVID BROWN   FROM: STUART OSTROW

Dear Ernie:

Beware. The earth has moved under the musical theater, (since "Hello, Young Lovers") and my disorientation is somewhere between Giacomo Puccini and Philip Glass. What I have attempted to do with your baby, Ernie, is to try making it sing. Your point about dropping Susan's suicide in favor of her knocking heads together is much better theater. (The screenplay alludes to her attempt being a set-up, but

as I said before, it's murky.) Whoever ultimately delivers this production should make particular use of Susan's trenchant novelette speech: "The terrible thing about people like you (Sidney) is that decent people have to become so much like you in order to stop you—in order to survive." I can hardly wait to hear Sidney's reply. What remains ambiguous, is what, and who, destroys Hunsecker? I've suggested it should be the disclosure of incest, by Susan, or Sidney, or both. Dallas' arm and teeth are all over the sidewalk (what can he do?), but Susan is motivated enough to exorcize the dybbuk in her soul—one hopes, in song. In order for this almost operatic (careful) moment to happen the love story must be improved. I put it to you: Is "Hasenpfeffer," (her pet name for Dallas) the stuff arias are made of? Is Susan going into the sunset, with Wingy Manone, to play club dates in Cleveland? The truth is Winchell did ruin BG by pressuring NBC-TV's "Broadway Open House," the new network late night talk show, not to use a Commie host. Jerry Lester got the job, and today BG has to beg press agent John Springer for comps to my opening nights. My primary interest in this tale is its modern musical subtext: the demise of pop songs and progressive 50s jazz, with the introduction of Rock n' Roll—coincidental with the end of an era, and the beginning of coarse, McCarthyite tactics to ruin lives. I think I know how to achieve this, or at least where to begin. There is a great deal to be settled before that happens, and please don't misunderstand, if I start, I'll need all the cheers I can get.

Stuart

To: David Brown

The Manhattan Project

888 Seventh Avenue

New York, NY 10106

4 November 1993

Dear David:

I've been trying to sort out my feelings after yesterday's telephone conversation with you. It was an earthquake. Obviously, you have been stewing, (no pun intended) about having asked me—and our subsequent agreement—to produce *The Sweet Smell Of Success*. You acknowledged I made it very clear from the beginning what my vision was, who I thought could write it, and why I, having produced many successful musicals, should be the captain of our skiff made of paper.

What you said yesterday was quite different. You thought you deserved first billing, but even if it meant not getting the musical on, you would never accept less than second. Furthermore, you, (and I assume,) Ernest Lehman, want more than consultation regarding the " integrity of the property. " David, everybody thinks you're a gent, so do I, but making a musical is a very tough job of command and since both of us now have doubts about our ability to work together I think it's best that I pass. Best of luck, to you, and Ernie.

Stuart

The musical version of *Sweet Smell of Success* opened in Chicago with the usual growing pains and ironically fell victim to the tabloid gossip it was singing about. (Walter Winchell's 1943 deadly column squib after the New Haven opening of Rodgers & Hammerstein's *Oklahoma!* decreed: "No gags, no girls, no chance.") Larry Gelbart quipped that if Hitler were alive the best torture would be to put him

out of town with a new musical. That was funny before *The Producers* arrived, however the part about pain is still pertinent. Critics, media gossips, theatre owners, family, friends, lovers, cynics, agents, lawyers, investors, and theatre party bookers, converge on Chicago, Boston, Washington, etc. (and New York during previews) wherever there's a new baby in town, and by offering their opinions instigate an internecine war between the parents of the new creation. It takes a deep-seated vision and strong leadership to persist in the face of disaster. The most important thing for the creators to remember during an out of town tryout is why they were initially excited about their concept. That is, if they have a concept.

13

ALAN MENKEN AND TOM EYEN

KICKS: THE SHOWGIRL MUSICAL

Several producers booted around *Kicks: The Showgirl Musical* by Alan Menken and Tom Eyen before Alan's agent offered it to me. I loved the score but Eyen's scattered storyline was a puzzle that would baffle a Buddha. It didn't help that Tom was convinced his book and lyrics to his first Broadway musical *Dreamgirls* was the sole reason for its success regardless of Michael Bennett's inspired direction and theatrical vision. Not. The composer Alan Menken (after *Little Shop Of Horrors* and before his Disney celebrity) created *Kicks* music that made me dance and I decided to produce it because of his prodigious talent. Wrong. Norman Lear was my partner and brought his recently formed Act III entourage to Eyen's trendy Horatio Street Village apartment for a listen-see audition. A disaster. Norman confirmed my worries regarding the musical's plot but deferred to the assumption I could make it work. Fuggedaboutit. I should have known it was impossible; like the day Jule Styne came to me with the idea of adapting the acclaimed movie *National Velvet* into a stage musical. "Just think of it, kid," said Jule, "Elizabeth Taylor and Mickey Rooney…" "But what do we do about the horses?" I interrupted. "…And MGM will put up all the dough," he continued. "But what about training the Pie to jump all those hedges?" I insisted. "…Plus, the topper is she's disguised as a boy and wins the race!!!!" Styne finished with a flourish. I pleaded: "Jule, how do we do the Grand National Steeplechase race on stage?" Without missing a beat he declared: "Don't worry about that kid, we'll fix it in rehearsals."

It's called the wishful thinking syndrome. Tom, who was also *Kicks'* director, wanted another workshop (A four-to-six week closed rehearsal with Equity actors cost, $250,000) to experiment with his book. Tom Eyen's writer-director experience was in small off off Broadway venues with shows such as *Why Hannah's Skirt Won't Stay Down*, *The Kama Sutra [An Organic Happening]*, *Lana Got Laid in Lebanon*

and *Women Behind Bars,* so the task of proving himself on Broadway, coupled with his obsession that Michael Bennett was merely his puppet on *Dreamgirls,* gave me pause. But what the hell I rationalized, in for a dollar, in for a quarter-million. Alarm bell.

To compensate for Eyen's inexperience with a large musical I hired Michael Smuin, the co-choreographer of *Sophisticated Ladies* and Hughes-Moss Casting to start auditioning actors on both coasts. What became immediately apparent to all of us (except Tom Eyen) was that the contradiction of being both author and director on a new musical destroys the collaboration process. How does our *Kicks* director tell our *Kicks* author his writing stinks? Siren. We closed in on casting the workshop company and I engaged Robin Wagner to design the show and rented the Minskoff rehearsal studio—all the while feeling everything was wrong. Why did I ignore all the warning signs in 1986? Looking back I realize it was my eagerness to get back on the boards—my last hit production was *Pippin* in 1972—and I had developed the typical Broadway self-importance known as hubris, a kind of high-flown insolence for every intractable rule that brings one some measure of success. It was only on the final day when casting the leading lady—an overweight Rockette who had all the best songs—that I asked Tom and Alan the question I should have asked on day one, the intense Jerry Robbins equalizer: What was the show about? There is no happy ending to this chapter.

I realized all Tom and Alan wanted from me was a meal ticket to redo their previous workshop with the same cast, so I withdrew and promised myself never to make the same mistake. Curiously, two years later, when we won the Best Play Tony Award for *M. Butterfly,* David Henry Hwang and I were on route to the press conference in Sardi's after the telecast when I saw Tom Eyen on 44th Street walking outside the Shubert Theatre. I turned to David and asked:

"David, what is our play about?" His reply was exactly the same at that triumphant moment as it was on the first day we decided to work together. Maybe that's the happy ending to *Kicks*. P.S.: A Broadway production of *Kicks* was always one of Scott Shukat's (Menken's agent) fondest wishes and when he called years later after Eyen was deceased and asked if I would reconsider producing it, I was momentarily thrilled at the prospect and said yes, provided Tom Eyen was really dead.

14
THE FLAMINGO KID

Carl Icahn knocked buster's block off and said that he was "elated by this grand victory for corporate governance." In other words Icahn, Blockbuster's largest shareholder, with a nearly 10 percent stake, and virtually no knowledge of the company's business and little relevant leadership experience, had tethered the board to his will. It's an old story and reminded me of my encounter with Icahn when he tried to apply his corporate raider talents to Broadway.

In 1987, my plan was to acquire The New Amsterdam Theatre (214 West 42nd Street) for the purpose of creating an American Musical Theatre and Opera Center for new works. "The New Amsterdam Center" would be organized as a limited partnership—capitalized at thirty million dollars—fifty percent of which would be financed by Carl Icahn, the other fifty percent by myself. Together, we would be would be the general partners, with the understanding that all artistic decisions would be mine alone. We were comfortable Bedford /Pound Ridge, New York neighbors then, walking the exclusive country club snow covered golf course and trading childhood memories.

He told how much like the movie character *The Flamingo Kid* he was in the forties: feeling boxed in his Queens home, in his life, in his dreams and how his eyes were opened to a world filled with what he saw as beautiful people and perfect lives, in affluent Forest Hills. Together we were kindred spirits from the Bronx and Queens and although I believed all boroughs are equal, I learned some are more equal than others. Our premiere musical would be a new original work, elaborate budgets were drawn, lawyers completed negotiations with the owners of the dilapidated 42nd Street property, I raised my half of the capitalization and a date was set to meet at Icahn & Co. to sign our agreement.

There were a dozen Rolex-watched Icahn executives in his board room, vetting titles and escrow payments, versus a lone general

manager and myself waiting for their check, when "The Flamingo Kid" finally arrived. He looked different without his Bedford galoshes and pea jacket but nothing prepared me for his change of attitude when he announced to all he had found a leading lady for "our musical." I reminded Icahn that casting actors was not the same as appointing board members or CEOs and we had previously agreed he had no understanding of the esoteric process. He replied something to the effect that if I didn't hire his singer/actress discovery the deal was off. It didn't make any sense; all the contract preparations, legal and accounting fees, media attention, forfeited for romance? It wasn't until he exited the room like a bad actor working for scale and his minions implored us that "it's not such a big deal," that I realized it was all a melodramatic deception to take control of the partnership. "Corporate governance" makes lousy art so I walked away from Icahn & Co. and continued producing new works by myself.

Not so incidentally, today Disney owns the crown jewel of 42nd Street and manufactures musicals for all who believe in happy endings. Too bad Carl blew controlling The New Amsterdam; he could have joined the present day landlord trend and rededicated it "The Carl Celian Icahn Theatre, Inc."

15

THE MUSICAL THEATRE LAB

In 1973, I had the impulse to originate a musical theatre laboratory and contributed a big chunk of my *Pippin* profits for the purpose of creating new musical theatre works. Although I was a lucky producer, I asked myself where would the musical theatre be in thirty years and would I have a job? Would the theatre still reflect the modern American spirit? Our ideas of beauty and justice, our love of fair chances and high aspirations, our self questionings and sweeping evaluations of our national life, our intrepid pursuit of dark insights as well as our cathartic laughter, our mockery, and a desire to free ourselves of constraints. When I told my lawyers and accountants the Stuart Ostrow Foundation, Inc., would have no proprietary rights in the works created they were incredulous and the theatre world was quick to co-opt the MTL process for commercial gain. As a result, the credo of every nonprofit organization today aspiring to " create musical theatre" is in reality thinking, "how much can we make from it?" Since I galvanized the monster it's only fitting I should attempt to restore its soul. When the SO Foundation negotiated the first "workshop" agreement with Actors Equity Association and originated the Musical Theatre Lab at St. Clements Church, our premiere musical was *The Robber Bridegroom* by Robert Waldman and Alfred Uhry, starring Raul Julia. (It went on to another life with John Housman's Acting Company starring Kevin Kline and Patti Lupone and a Broadway production with Barry Bostwick.) Much has been attributed to the workshop process originated at St. Clements; developed at the Kennedy Center, Harvard, University of Houston, and now productive at The Hobby Center for the Performing Arts in Houston. The founding SOF Board of Directors were: Ingram Ash, Jerry Bock, Edgar Bronfman, Schuyler Chapin, Bob Fosse, Goddard Lieberson, William Safire, and Stephen Sondheim.

Since its inception the Musical Theatre Lab produced some forty experimental musicals, some distinguished, yet all dedicated to creators seeing how far they could take their work, as opposed to seeing how much they could make from it. It was a place where Maurice Sendak, the famous artist, and Carole King, the pop songwriter, created *Really Rosie* and playwright Arthur Miller wrote lyrics for Stanley Silverman's music to *Up From Paradise*. The MTL also gave the first American commission to Robert Wilson, to produce a musical work based on *Medea*.

These "gypsy run-throughs" were rehearsed with Actors Equity Association members (at a sixth of weekly union-scale salary) for four weeks and performed five times over an additional two-week period, with six days rewriting time after the second performance. No reviews were permitted. They were performed with no scenery, no lighting, in rehearsal clothes, with makeshift props, and were accompanied by one piano. This was done for several reasons—to emphasize improving the material more than presenting a finished production, and to allow no limitations as to size of cast and style of production.

When Michael Bennett came to St. Clements, he thought he was in heaven. The realization of rehearsing and performing a new musical inexpensively was just what he needed in order to implement his concept of a musical about Broadway gypsy-dancers. He went to the nonprofit Public Theatre and together with Joe Papp applied to Equity for the MTLab formula and mounted *A Chorus Line*. Rehearsing for a year at bargain basement prices Michael would record the ambitions, secrets, and disappointments of various Broadway gypsies (many from *Pippin*) until he had a text and score. The results were stunning and one of the great ripoffs of the actor's union; which prompted the landlord of the Sam S. Shubert

Ostrow, 'Pippin' Producer, Funds Musical Theater Workshop

By MEL GUSSOW

With $120,000 of his profits from the hit Broadway musical "Pippin," the producer Stuart Ostrow has started the nonprofit Stuart Ostrow Foundation, "to advance the education and development of musical theater in the United States.

Mr. Ostrow plans to increase the funding and eventually to make the foundation, through his support, and that of government, and other, foundations and the public, into a $1.5-million institution.

The major thrust of the foundation is to create a "musical theater lab." In a pilot program in collaboration with Theater at St. Clement's, the experimental Off Off Broadway company under the artistic direction of Kevin O'Connor, the Ostrow Foundation will present workshop productions of five new musicals during the 1974-75 season. The program is budgeted at $32,000, half of that provided as a matching grant by the foundation. The Ostrow Foundation

also has plans to provide seed money to musical productions that are having difficulty in raising funds and creative individuals (including a producer) will be gathered together in a workshop for a week of preproduction.

For each musical, various creative individuals (including composers, lyricists, directors, choreographers, producers, and authors. Future musical-theater education programs in conjunction with the State University at Purchase are also projected.

'Out-of-Town Situation'

In addition to Mr. Ostrow, the foundation's board members are Stephen Sondheim, Bob Fosse, Jerry Bock, Edgar Bronfman, Goddard Lieberson and Ingram Ash.

According to Mr. O'Connor, the St. Clement's workshops will create "an out-of-town situation in town," without an enormous outlay of money. (productions will cost $3,000 instead of $600,000) and bridge the gap between back-

without facing critical and commercial pressures.

For each musical, various creative individuals (including an opportunity to write— and to rewrite shows.

Mr. Ostrow said that among the people he would like to have participate are Richard Peaslee, Kenneth Cavandar, Paul Simon, Joe Raposo "and kids out of Carnegie Tech, where Stephen Schwartz [who wrote "Pippin"] came from," Mr. O'Connor added that he would also like to attract "playwrights who verge on the musical theater," such as Leonard Melfi and Julie Bovasso, to write for the musical theater.

"Stuart and I are a very interesting combination," Mr. O'Connor said. As actor and director, Mr. O'Connor is one of the prime forces behind the Off Off Broadway movement. At St. Clement's he has presented work by in-

novative companies like the Open Theater and the Bread and Puppet Theater, as well as original plays—which will continue next season in addition to the musical series. Mr. Ostrow is known as a profit-making Broadway producer (of "1776" as well as "Pippin").

Together with a project coordinator still to be chosen, they will share the artistic responsibility for the musical workshops. Each emphasized the latitude of the projected work and the need for encouraging musical artists.

"The musical is the most popular art form in this country," said Mr. Ostrow. "We've got to replenish our treasury. We've got to find new people, to encourage new writing for the musical theater."

Playwrights Sought

The lab is designed to offer creators of musicals an opportunity that is now more easily available to playwrights Off Off Broadway. "Everyone does readings of plays, but not musicals," Mr. O'Connor said. The St. Clement's program is intended to

ing auditions and full productions. Participants will have an opportunity to write—

Notwithstanding our efforts, Broadway produced only three new hit musicals in five seasons, from 1976–1981, compared to four new hit musicals (in one season) in 1950. We were going bankrupt. Why wasn't the theatre establishment doing something about replenishing the treasury of American musicals? Was I the sole source of nonprofit funding? I tried my best by restoring the endangered purpose of the Musical Theatre Lab; moving it from the Kennedy Center to Harvard-Radcliffe, and from commercial management (my fault, I fear) back to artistic experimentation. Steve Sondheim cautioned me, "Academia equals stasis equals death," but I rationalized about Harvard because Robert Brustein, founding director of the Yale Repertory and Harvard's American Repertory theaters, became my Rabbi, championed the Lab's mission and made me an adjunct professor. We managed to produce two successful workshops:

American Passion (Willie Young, Fred Burch) 1983, Agassiz House, Harvard/Radcliffe, Cambridge.
Crosstown Bus (Bruce Detrick), 1984, Agassiz House, Harvard/Radcliffe, Cambridge.

For a decade, the Musical Theatre Lab was a throwback to the Mickey and Judy "let's put on a show" films, and new actors, singers, and dancers on the block vied to perform in a MTL workshop. They included John Goodman, Tisha Campbell, Robert Downey Jr., Todd Graff, Jane Krakowski, Martha Plimpton, Laura Dean, Terry Quinn, Kathy Moss, Cass Morgan, Fred Coffin, and Austin Pendleton—all working for $250 a week, plus sharing a double room at the cheapest motel in Boston or Washington. By then however, my donations to the Lab had been expended and precious few philanthropic organizations thought the musical theatre needed help. After all, wasn't Cats making millions? I also became disenchanted with the NEA and

it's politicizing of grant awards and heeded board member William Safire's warning that government didn't belong in the arts, ergo we had to close down.

In 1995 I accepted The University of Houston's offer to be the Cynthia Woods Mitchell Distinguished Professor of Theatre Chair, which included a laboratory for new musicals in return for joining Edward Albee and Jose Quintero as a member of the School of Theatre faculty. I now had a venue for the dormant Musical Theatre Lab and what followed was:

> *Doll* (Michael Korie, Scott Frankel). 1995, University of Houston, Wortham Theatre.
> *Coyote Goes Salmon Fishing* (Deborah Baley Brevoort, Scott Davenport Richards). 1996, University of Houston, Wortham Theatre.
> *1040* (Jerry Bock, Jerry Sterner). 1997, University of Houston, Wortham Theatre.
> *'Twas...* (Tom Bähler, Guy Toubes). 2001, University of Houston, Wortham Theatre.

The crucial problem with the creation of new musicals is the lack of musical dramatists. Therefore, I expanded the MTL mission to include:

> University of Houston
> School of Theatre
> Musical Theatre Collaboration Class Fall Interviews
> THEA 4335
> THEA 6338
> The Musical Theatre Collaboration Class.

Three teams; consisting of graduate, undergraduate, and nonmatric-
ulating UH eligible composers, lyricists, book writers, directors, producers, choreographers, designers, and stage managers, are chosen by
Stuart Ostrow each fall semester. Each team is assigned a risky under-
lying work to be musicalized, and are nurtured and encouraged to
learn the necessary give and take of the crucial writing/collaborative
process. At the end of the semester, the Musical Theatre Lab Class
performs excerpts from all three newly created musicals for an
enlightened Houston audience in Zilkha Hall at The Hobby Center
For The Performing Arts.

Composers: may perform their compositions live, or submit
a tape and/or score of their work intended for musical theatre,
opera, pop music, symphonic/chamber/choral, or any other vocal or
instrumental form that conveys the human condition.

Lyricists and Librettists: may submit examples of their
work, intended for musical theatre, opera, or pop music, or as poetry expressed in verse, song, or rhyme.

Book writers: may submit original plays, musicals, novels,
tales, newspaper articles, reviews, diary, etc.; any writing that tells or
dramatizes a story.

Directors & Choreographers: may present a scene, musical
number, or staged dance, from any play, musical, or ballet. Each
applicant must provide his or her own cast, and accompanist.

Designers: show portfolio; including models of sets and
costume swatches, if available.

Producers: should show evidence of their ability to be hard-
headed, soft-hearted, cautious, reckless, a hopeful innocent in fair
weather, a stern pilot in stormy weather, a mathematician who prefers
to ignore the laws of mathematics and trust intuition, an idealist, a
realist, a practical dreamer, a sophisticated gambler, a stage-struck child.

Stage Managers: must aspire to be Producers. Submit c.v.

In 1995, the Musical Theatre Lab presented excerpts from
The Piebald, The Incredible Shrinking Man, Man's Fate.
1996, *Boule de Suif, Random Harvest, Show Biz Connections.*
1997, *Ring 'Round the Moon, The Count of Monte Cristo, Moon for
the Misbegotten.*
1998, *Madame Bovary, Crossing Delancey, Tuesdays' with Morrie.*
1999, *Frida, Diego and Rockefeller, The Man Who Mistook His Wife
for a Hat, Petronius, Three Cornered Hat.*
2000, *Young Goodman Brown, The Mandrake, Ship of Fools.*
2001, *Babette's Feast, Steel Magnolias, The Admirable Crichton.*
2002, *The Color of Water, Casablanca, A Confederacy of Dunces.*
2003, *Life of Pi, Magic Mountain, Nicholas and Alexandria.*
2004, *The Wonderful Ice Cream Suit, Time Remembered,
The Lovely Bones.*

Present at the creation, leaping in the dark and going against the
grain, indeed. The story goes on—at least until my next Broadway
musical gets written. Until then, the best way I know to resuscitate
the theatre is to produce dangerous new works.

16

THE PRODUCER'S NEW CLOTHES

What does a producer do? The textbook reply is: The writer designs and builds the boat. The director is the captain of the boat and responsible for sailing it. The producer is the head of the steamship line, which has hired them to protect his investment and arrive safely across the ocean. Baloney, corporate thinking. Risk-taking individuals today in America are in short supply, which is why the legendary heroes of our past are selling so many books. There is a yearning in the national psyche to live life dangerously but instead of leaping in the dark we sit in it, watching *Lord of the Rings* and *Pirates of the Caribbean*. Alas, being an individual entrepreneur, lone gun, stubborn independent is no longer possible. Producing committees seldom reach a decision on anything, which is one reason theatre today is aimless and stranded at sea. Inexperienced producers with lots of money to gamble are lured into showbiz for the shallow glitter and hype of media billing, opening night parties, stage auditions (especially the dance calls) and yes, the shabby custom of hitting on actors in the cast.

Recently a fledgling producer with a show in rehearsals asked me what to do about his director who wouldn't listen to any suggestions from the creative team. I told him, *Support the director until the moment you're compelled to replace him.* That's what a producer must do because he or she alone has the power to change the course of events in order to prevent a shipwreck. Notwithstanding the Dramatists Guild and Society of Stage Directors and Choreographers contracts: *power equals money equals rule.* However, the producer cannot be a despot just because he controls the purse strings. He must have a vision of what the show is about and the talent and erudition to convince the creators to remain on course and remember why they were initially excited about their concept. If they don't have a concept they should close the show and return the unused cost of the production

to the investors. How many producers today would consider applying that old-fashioned principle? The answer is, too few, and the result is an appalling increase in flop musicals and plays opening on Broadway. If more producers had the courage to close their turkeys out-of-town, those productions who brave the storm and are worthy of a port in New York will be celebrated and ipso facto, raise the level of artistic excellence along the once Great White Way.

Attention also must be paid to the alarming notion that words no longer belong in the theatre. This, quoting a flourishing Broadway producer, from the *New York Times*: "...the most successful shows appeal even to non–English-speakers, who make up a significant portion of the Broadway audience. To compare it (*The Producers*) to *Cats* or *The Lion King* isn't fair because it's a funny but literate piece of theatre that's language-dependent. It's not pure visual or musical entertainment, and those are the types of shows that last 15 or 20 years." WARNING! Without words, theatre is Las Vegas; drama is silent, characters dumb, catharsis crippled, dénouement and metaphor at a standstill. Words, dialogue, lyrics, are companions, teachers, magicians, without which the development of the theatre would have been impossible. For example, the gypsy run-through spoke the essential language of the theatre. On the last Saturday after five weeks of rehearsals in Manhattan, the day before a play or musical left for an out-of-town tryout, they had a gypsy run-though; Broadway jargon for a private performance of a new work attended by the cast members' family and friends. It took place in a dark theatre or large empty space where the newborn creation was performed with no scenery, no lighting, in rehearsal clothes, with makeshift props, and accompanied by one piano. Purpose? To help the creators and actors discover where the laughs were and where they weren't, where the songs soared and where they fell flat, and where the drama compelled

and where it bored their nearest and dearest to sleep. *Musicals aren't written, they're rewritten.* The staging wasn't about falling chandeliers, puppets, or hairdos. It was about the words, music, dance and drama. The actors provided a plank and a passion and the audience provided the power of imagination.

More often than not it was magic. It would be weeks of living in crummy hotels and drafty theaters in Philadelphia, Boston, or Washington before the company would experience the same thrill—what with adjusting to all the theatrical window dressing of backdrops and stage traps, lighting focus sessions, crowded dressing rooms, makeup, and orchestra rehearsals. The creators and cast however, wary of the Emperor's New Clothes, maintained belief in their musical by summoning up the memory of the gypsy run-through until they got their show back. Unfortunately too many of today's spectacular productions are imagined by theatre scoundrels who believe with a loom, silk and gold thread they can dress a musical into creation—merely to be confronted by the genius of an audience who can only see things as their eyes show them—to know the musical is naked. The practice of fixing the show out-of-town is long past because the huge cost of the physical production today locks in the creators of a new musical to its scenery. Can you imagine the *Wicked* producers cutting the floating mechanical bubble and winged monkey who levitates over the audience rather than fixing, what Ben Brantley termed "generically impassioned songs…in a bloated production that might otherwise spend close to three hours flapping its oversized wings without taking off." No, the gimmicks cost too much, so sadly, they book the theatre, cast the lead, raise the money, and build the scenery, rather than insisting the musical be written first. Too much money following too little concept. It wasn't an actor who said "The show must go on," it was a producer.

Once upon a time, there were producers who amassed millions in the theatre. When the Great Depression erased their profits they could have retired, individually wealthy and secure. Instead, they came to an inexplicable decision. They determined to keep the theatre alive. They poured their own money onto the gamble. Almost alone they kept the marquee lights burning; stubborn men fought to save the stage. Why? Perhaps because in these men, there was a passion for the form. Somehow they reacted to the beauty, the poetry, the art. They loved.

THE PRODUCER'S NEW CLOTHES

17

COMES THE REVOLUTION!

In contrast to Europe, where even the victors lay exhausted and destitute, the United States emerged from World War II with a renewed sense of confidence. At the same time, the inescapable truths of the war darkened the imaginations of thoughtful people. Extreme pessimism and extreme optimism suddenly appeared equally justified. Not surprisingly, the scale of art in New York began to change and expand; anything, artists began to feel, was possible and throughout the late forties and fifties that exhilaration generated the last great era of theatre producers. Not the Mel Brooks parody, but the real thing: Bobby Griffith, Hal Prince, David Merrick, Saint Subber, Lemuel Ayers, Kermit Bloomgarden, Robert Whitehead, Richard Barr, Herman Shumlin, The Theatre Guild, Feuer & Martin, Cheryl Crawford, Mike Todd, Jean Dalrymple, Leland Hayward, Alfred de Liagre, Jr., The Playwrights' Company, Herman Levin, Jed Harris, Max Gordon, Irene M. Selznick, Gilbert Miller, Alex Cohen, Robert Fryer, and Roger Stevens, all put their *toches ahfen tish!* (literally, asses on the table!) and enriched the Broadway theatre with the likes of *West Side Story, Look Back in Anger, Gypsy, The Tenth Man, Kiss Me Kate, Death of a Salesman, The Diary of Anne Frank, Guys and Dolls, Mister Roberts, South Pacific,* and *A Streetcar Named Desire*; surely an amazing contribution for one decade.

Today the theatre must compete with movies, television, and the Internet to capture an audience and there are too few stage-struck theatre producers around to nurture new works. A. J. Jacobs, a young, hip New Yorker writes about why he doesn't care about the theatre: "Whenever I'm at a Broadway show, I keep waiting for the director to cut to a new scene. Where's the montage? Where's the extreme close-up featuring the actor's huge, unblinking eyes? Instead I'm looking at the exact sawed-in-half house for an entire excruciating hour." Of course. How can the theatre compete with a film like

Eternal Sunshine of the Spotless Mind, a beautiful romance which takes place almost entirely inside of one man's head, or the movie comedy *Sideways* where a character is such a loser he steals money from his mother? Answer: not unless it discovers the likes of Charlie Kaufman, whose story is festive like happiness, buoyant like romance, fiery like a new love, and shattered like a broken heart, or Alexander Payne and Jim Taylor, who co-authored the comic tale of two men hunting wine country for true love and the perfect pinot noir.

We've lost today's best and the brightest writers to films, not only because the silver screen pays better and reaches a gigantic international audience but because they are unwilling to put up with the hocus-pocus of the theatre. It's too much bother of a boring nature to fight with the money, and the real estate, and the guilds, national arts councils, and the foundations, to get a play on the boards—never mind the unions and the frauds and all-around incompetents who from sheer force of ambition occupy all the positions of power, and prevent, obstruct, neutralize, distort, or otherwise prohibit the possibility of a new, original work being produced. Comes the revolution, the theatre will abandon the establishment in order to survive. New writers, directors, choreographers and designers, will participate internationally via the Internet to create a musical or play just for the credit and recognition, in much the same way software is created for Linux or Apache by eager young computer visionaries. Imagine how many more investors will find the theatre a profitable venture without having to pay royalties constituting one third of the weekly operating costs! If we are ever to have another golden era for Broadway we must heed Willem de Kooning: "You have to change to stay the same."

18
ONE MORE TIME

Rehearsals for the theatre are unique. Unlike solemnizing weddings or a state occasion it is the dramatic act of giving life to a make-believe story. Where the interpreters must suspend reality and imagine Chicago and Charlemagne dancing, Sir Thomas More and Jean Valjean praying, The Demon Barber of Fleet Street cutting throats in his sweatpants, and tomcats, pussycats, tabbycats, and chessycats in leotards transporting Grizabella into cat heaven. "I'm trying to make it work" is the love that has the blood singing during rehearsals; when the director or choreographer fixes a number and suddenly the musical is off the ground. It happened when Jerome Robbins had Anna (Gertrude Lawrence) teach the King (Yul Brynner) how to clog-step, in "Shall We Dance?" Neither could retain the rhythm so Robbins used the three after-beats of the song's musical phrase to emphasize the necessity of keeping in step; and as the actors gained confidence, a/k/a rehearsal, it became a show-stopping demonstration of their ability to fly!

Rehearsals of a new show took place in a Spartan space, perhaps to emphasize that theatre is a plank and a passion, but more likely because the producer is a cheapskate. Broadway Arts (*Pippin*) had one bathroom for a cast of thirty, the New Amsterdam Theatre (*The Most Happy Fella*) roof leaked on stage, (*The Music Man*) space above Ratner's Deli smelled of potato latkes and knishes—not the preeminent aroma for a musical about River City, Iowa—and at 890 Broadway (*M. Butterfly*) you had to walk five blocks during a snowstorm from your parking garage to the building. In spite of it all, these alternating drafty, overheated, grimy, windowless, often lit by an on-stage ghost light, quarters were the magical theatrical incubators for their nervous creators and casts. It was where the great John Dexter discovered a flaw in his staging of David Henry Hwang's meditation on men and women, East and West, appearance and real-

ity. There was no dramatization of how the duped French diplomat and his lover—a male communist spy masquerading as a female Chinese opera singer—had sex. "How could he not know?" was the question that stretched audience credulity until the skillful Dexter had B. D. Wong mount an unseen John Lithgow and, ever so delicately, start to pleasure him. It was an exquisite, tasteful moment, which nevertheless had voyeurs during the tryout in Washington walk out shouting "Shame!" at the stage. Happily, Broadway audiences proved to be less provincial.

Of course more failures come out of rehearsals than successes. Here's why: a cast of 5 to 50 strangers are thrust together for four weeks, rehearsing 7 out of 10 hours daily (10 out of 12 the last week) dancing, dehydrating, singing, acting, eating, resting, arguing, loving, and despairing. As for the creative team, every one of them has a different priority. The writers want to hear their words—what Tom Stoppard calls "clarity of utterance," the composers beg for vocal intonation and volume, stars demand sea-changes in the book and score, the director dotes on his favorite actors and tortures others, the choreographer's dance combinations accentuate tits and ass, and the producers are off planning the opening night party. No one is in charge. Rare, good times come when everyone connected with the production is doing the same show. Then rehearsal accidents become providential. For example, during the Act II rehearsals for Frank Loesser's *The Most Happy Fella*, when Robert Weede, in a wheelchair, and Jo Sullivan, his younger mail-order bride (Tony and Rosabella) discover they truly love each other after Tony patronizes her: "Ma, omma old enough to be you papa," and she replies: "I'm no baby—I know what I know/And I know it's my plan/Just to love you/Like a woman loves a wonderful man." As the introduction to "My Heart is So Full of You" sneaks in and then crescendos, Tony

begins to rise shouting with great joy: "Quanto sono contento! Cosa ti posse dire? Tu mi stai a cuore! What can I say? What can I say!" and was directed to slump back into the wheelchair as Rosabella wheels him downstage for their duet. Instead, Weede stood up, threw away his cane, embraced Jo and together they walked (he limped) downstage in tempo to the thrilling refrain of the song. Of course it stayed in the show. When the director Joseph Anthony asked Robert Weede, a reserved 20-year opera luminary starring in his first Broadway musical, what possessed him to improvise, he replied, "Isn't that what Tony would do?" Anthony nodded; they were doing the same show.

Inevitably there comes a time when you have to stop rehearsing and face the real world, but the transition isn't easy. Bob Fosse said he could fix his life if he had more rehearsal time. Fortunately he enjoyed better luck in the theatre. One day during rehearsals of *Pippin* at the recently completed Kennedy Center, a terrified Roger Stevens called me to get the company out of the theatre because there was a bomb threat! I ran from the Watergate Hotel to the Opera House and found the company and Fosse deep into a new ten-minute number for the finale of the show. So as not to panic the cast, I whispered in Bob's ear that we had to evacuate the building immediately; "... there's a bomb about to go off." Fosse blinked, then turned to the company and said: "O.K. kids, just one more time."

AFTERWORD

A PLACE TO BEGIN AGAIN

Once upon a time in America there were musicals that revolutionized the way we told stories by way of song and dance. *Lady in the Dark, Oklahoma! Annie Get Your Gun, Kiss Me Kate, Guys and Dolls, My Fair Lady, West Side Story, Fiddler on the Roof, A Chorus Line.* The creators of such abundance included Kurt Weill & Ira Gershwin, Rodgers & Hammerstein, Irving Berlin, Cole Porter, Frank Loesser, Lerner & Loewe, Leonard Bernstein, Stephen Sondheim, and Bock & Harnick. But—more than 50 years later in some cases—we are still trying to grow musicals from that well-plowed field. We are eating our seed corn. In the 1920s that began with the ending of WWI and closed with the beginning of the Depression, the musical theatre flourished because a new generation of songwriters was waiting in the wings. From 1930–1950 the economic pinch of the depression, the gathering war clouds of Europe and WWII generated even more new writers and developed the art form. In the fifties the parameters of the American musical theatre were five blocks long by about one and a half blocks wide; from forty-fourth to forty-ninth Streets, between Eighth Avenue and Broadway. Dinty Moore's and Sardi's restaurants were the club hangouts and the League of New York Theatres was a loose confederation of enlightened, talented, risk-taking Broadway producers and a few passive theatre landlords who periodically negotiated collective bargaining agreements with the actors', musicians', and stagehands' unions.

It was an exciting cottage industry with lots of old-fashioned kickbacks, extortion, and patronage for those who played the management-labor game. The average musical cost $150,000 to produce and the price of a ticket was $7. There were as many as ninety attractions electric-lighted on Broadway in one season and it was not uncommon for sixteen of them to be new musicals. The New York middle-class audience went to the theatre at least five times a year—

new productions were prolific and hit songs from Broadway musicals were heard everywhere. The reign of Irving Berlin, Cole Porter, and Rodgers and Hammerstein was nearly over. Loesser, Lerner and Loewe, Bernstein, Comden and Green, and Jule Styne, all of whom started in the late forties were at the peak of their creativity with *Guys and Dolls, Wonderful Town, My Fair Lady, and Gypsy*, but it was the new kids on the block who would set the pace for the next generation. Dick Adler and Jerry Ross wrote *The Pajama Game*, and *Damn Yankees*, back-to-back hits; twenty-seven-year-old lyricist Stephen Sondheim's collaborations with Leonard Bernstein and Jule Styne were auspicious: Jerry Bock's and Sheldon Harnick's *Fiorello!* won the Pulitzer Prize; and Meredith Willson marched into town with *The Music Man*.

Fortunately for the musical theatre what also was at work during this period was the apprentice-mentor tradition, an indispensable process (nowadays extinct) by which you learned your craft from an experienced and trusted counselor. George Abbott trained his second assistant stage manager, Harold Prince, Stephen Sondheim was a gofer on *Allegro,* for Oscar Hammerstein II, and I plugged songs for Frank Loesser. In the 50s music publishers like Chappell & Co., Buddy Morris, and Tommy Valando, augmented the role of mentoring by identifying talented, aspiring songwriters—paying them a modest advance on their future royalties and providing a piano and a place to meet. A place to begin. The best was Frank Music Corp. which was fast becoming a salon for Broadway composers and lyricists: Adler and Ross, *The Pajama Game, Damn Yankees*, Wright and Forrest, *Kismet, Grand Hotel,* Moose Charlap, *Peter Pan, Whoop Up,* Meredith Willson, *The Music Man, The Unsinkable Molly Brown,* and of course Loesser himself with *Where's Charley?* and *Guys and Dolls.* It was bedlam at 119 West 57th Street in New York; one team of writers following another into the only piano room on the floor. You

could hear Carolyn Leigh and Charlap cawing, "I've Got To Crow," all the way down the block to the Russian Tea Room and listen at the locked door to Loesser composing "Project #3," a code name for *The Most Happy Fella.*

It was in this creative incubator that I was hatched and discovered how crucial collaboration is for the creation of musical theatre. When composer Jerry Ross died unexpectedly after their second smash hit *Damn Yankees,* Adler tried writing both words and music but the chemistry wasn't the same. During *The Pajama Game* tryout, Dick and Jerry were closeted in the New Haven's Taft Hotel, with second act problems. Bob Fosse had asked for a big new dance number, a tango, for Carol Haney. It was past midnight and nothing was coming. "Olé..." said Ross in mock desperation to Adler. "Thanks a lot," Adler mumbled. Finally, an exhausted Adler spoke: "The only thing I can think of is a title—Hernando's Hideaway." "Why that?" asked Ross. "Because it rhymes with Olé," Adler replied. They wrote the entire song in two hours: "I know a dark secluded place/A place where no one knows your face/A glass of wine, a fast embrace/It's called Hernando's hideaway/Olé!" Chemistry.

The Broadway musical theatre in its wild and glittering maelstrom of opulence and extravagance will not evade the profound effects of September 11, 2001, indeed the catastrophe may have declared its need for revolution. Where are the producers who will subsidize the new writers? How many investors and theatre owners will put money into risky shows? Who is willing to save Broadway? Producers outnumber their casts today. They are a consortium, a corporation, or a gathering of landlords and are ridiculed as charlatans. (Livent/Drabinsky, Melvin Kaminsky—a burlesque not Shakespeare nor Fielding, but Minsky.) And it's all about money. Today's multi-million dollar marriage between Broadway musicals and Las Vegas

was inevitable; more tricked out scenery and dumb-downed (90 minutes) content in order to market more weekly performances. Early Vegas attempts to truncate two-hours-plus musicals were rejected by the classy, principled writers of their time. It was said Rodgers and Hammerstein turned down a rich offer for *Carousel* after The Sands Hotel and Casino suggested their "Soliloquy" in Act One be shortened as follows: "Bill... My boy Bill I will see that he is named after me…. or die!" What is deeply wrong with sin city's lust for profits is that it will tempt Broadway to produce other mindless musicals. Indeed the president of the League of American Theaters and Producers boasts that Broadway has become the Las Vegas type of popular entertainment currency! One can only imagine the essential artistic coinage for the next Broadway-on-route to Vegas musical: a mother, a daughter and three possible dads in white suits, on roller skates, doing the New York Hustle in a tiny Greek island disco to a score by Jay-Z.

The greatest question musical dramatists must answer is: does the story I am telling sing? Is the subject sufficiently off the ground to compel the heightened emotion of bursting into song? Will a song add a deeper understanding of character or situation? (When I recently played a recording of Frank Loesser show tunes for my 21-year-old University seminar students, they thought it was classical music.) It's no wonder the indigenous American art form has not evolved and that the young, new musical theatre composers, lyricists, and book writers are searching for an original voice. We can make the earth move again if we teach writers that the way to write a great musical is to be great. The way to write a poor musical is to be thinking of getting rich.

I propose a concept to establish *The Institute for Advanced Study in Musical Theatre.* An independent, private institution dedicated entirely

to the encouragement, support and patronage of learning through fundamental research and definitive scholarship. Inspired by the Bamberger families and Abraham Flexner's 1933 creation of *The Institute for Advanced Study*, in Princeton Township, New Jersey, it will be a center where artistic and intellectual inquiry can be carried out in the most favorable circumstances. The Institute would be home to some of the most highly regarded creators and thinkers of the 21st century, drawing promising young composers, lyricists, book writers, directors, choreographers, producers, designers, postdocs and accomplished senior scholars from around the world to its campus.

The establishment of *The Institute for Advanced Study in Musical Theatre*, a think-tank for musical theatre creators, will offer freedom and collaboration to professional Senior and Junior Fellows from the international theatre community. They will be invited to inquire into the unknown, each to be selected on the basis of a specific project, concept, and/or goal for their fellowship. The Institute would consist of the Society of Musical Theatre Dramatists, the Society of Musical Theatre Directors and Choreographers, the Society of Musical Theatre Producers, and the Society of Musical Theatre Designers. Each entity would have a small permanent Faculty, and Senior and Junior fellowships awarded annually to visiting members from the international professional theatre community and universities throughout the world. The Institute would have no formal curriculum, degree programs, and schedule of courses, laboratories, or other experimental facilities. It would be committed to exploring the most fundamental areas of knowledge and artistic creation, areas where there is little expectation of immediate outcomes or striking applications—nevertheless, the long-term impact of the Institute research will sometimes be dramatic. No contracted or directed research will be done at the Institute, and it would receive no income

from tuition or fees. Resources for operations will come from endowment income, grants from private foundations and gifts from corporations and individuals, nor will it have any formal links to the professional theatre or any educational institution. (As with Caesar's wife, the Institute must be above suspicion.) It should be a haven where musical theatre professionals and scholars could regard the world as their laboratory, without being carried off in the maelstrom of the immediate. It should provide the facilities, and the time requisite to fundamental inquiry into the unrevealed. A place to begin again.

I imagine the Institute to be a kind of intellectual hotel for dramatists, directors and choreographers, producers, and designers; who want to understand everything to know and explain the whole of musical theatre creation. Where book writers, lyricists, composers, MTV creators along with novelists, poets, and journalists investigate what it means to dramatize stories that sing. Where directors and choreographers from musical theatre, ballet, opera, post-modernist and hip-hop cultures explore new ways to theatricalize joy and sorrow. Where experienced and aspiring producers examine the culture of the 21st century as it applies to musical subjects, and where CEOs from other industries study to improve the artistic, business and financial structure of mounting productions internationally. And where designers, architects, painters and computer animators probe new technologies for creative and cost-efficient ways to realize the scenic/visual components of a musical. Far from being a refuge of placidity out in the woods, the Institute should live in the real world of downtown urban life; surrounded by theaters, concert halls, museums, libraries, universities, cultural centers, art galleries, clubs, movie houses, hotels and restaurants. For our Senior and Junior Fellows, I want the best men and women in the world—paraphrasing from

Edward Regis' *Who Got Einstein's Office*—"to create tension on the premises, a crackle in the air. What the ideally perfect Institute needs more than anything else are one or two prickly pears to balance out all the harmony and concordance. The Institute needs some dissonance, some thunder, and some strangeness in the proportion, some crazy people. It also needs its Great Ancients, its old men shuffling through the hallways, and nodding off on an afternoon. In a way, these living icons are the most important people of all: they are the musical theatre's memory, its link to the past, a vision of Golden Ages far away and long ago. For them the Institute is—and in fact ought to be—a great reward, a Toyland."

Arguably, the Musical Theatre Lab in 1973 was the singular workshop process until Michael Bennett made it a chorus line. Since then too many writers have used presentation as their reason for existence; in my opinion to avoid having to first solve the dramaturgy on paper. Blocked? Get a workshop! Theory is not the enemy. I believe to be learned in an art, the Theory is sufficient; to be a master of it, both the Theory and practice are requisite. In an age where everything is Great precisely because nothing is very good, there's something rational about a think-tank for musical theatre in this absurd time. The sign above the door (courtesy of Stephen Sondheim) will read: "Where is style?/Where is skill?/Where is forethought?/Where's discretion of the heart/Where's passion in the art/ Where's craft?" Rather than the current factory mentality, I would encourage these sequestered writers, directors, producers and designers to do what comes naturally, without the pressure of having to produce a bigger and better widget. An out-of-town salon if you will; terrific accommodations, food, company, stimulation, workspace, a salary, and a piano. Ambitious? Yes. Achievable? For a song.

EPILOGUE

"WHAT IS IT ABOUT?"

Somerset Maugham ended *The Summing Up* with a solution: "The beauty of life is nothing but this, that each should act in conformity with his nature and his business." In a *Variety* interview celebrating the Shubert Organization's 100th anniversary, its lawyer-cum-chairman speaking of their production of *Jerome Robbins' Broadway,* summoned up his experience with the renowned director-choreographer: "That was three years of working with one of the most difficult men," he recalls of Robbins. "Defensively aggressive. You could never get any satisfaction from that man under any circumstances. He treated his dancers horribly. And yet, if he gave them a compliment—'That was very good!'—they were in ecstasy." Fortunately none of Robbins' historical producers—Leland Hayward, Rodgers and Hammerstein, Harold S. Prince, The Theatre Guild, nor David Merrick—ever felt the need to pass judgment on his genius, nor Robbins' methods to achieve purity of line and extension from his dancers; and their collaborations flourished. One also may understand, but not forgive, Arthur Laurents' recent bashing of Robbins in his memoir—after all, they collaborated on two of the most successful works in the Broadway musical canon, *West Side Story* and *Gypsy* and time heals all wounds, unless you pick at them—nevertheless they both were artists. With regard to the Shuberts, their nature was business; Jerome Robbins' nature was art. Q.E.D. When Jerome Robbins and I worked on *We Take the Town, The Apple Tree,* and *A Pray by Blecht* the first and last question he always asked was: "What is it about?" Our three creative teams never answered the question to his satisfaction, so he withdrew, and none of the musicals ever achieved its potential. Of course Jerry was difficult—demanding would be more accurate. He insisted on quality. In a culture dominated by commercialism directed to popular consumption, can Broadway ever again cultivate an environment where a degree of quality is possible? In order to do so, it must first answer Robbins' question.

INDEX

INDEX

157